Praise for *Stick to Your Vision* and Wes Williams

"'Stick to Your Vision' and '416/905' were legendary moments in my life, not to mention this man's career. Those two songs let me know that it was possible to make a city so far removed feel like it was a part of it all. Now every song and move I make I think about my people back home and how proud I am of them and they are of me. I owe a part of my confidence as a rapper to Maestro."

— Drake (Singer/Songwriter)

"It's an honour and a privilege to write these words of support for the 'Godfather of Canadian Hip Hop' Wesley Williams and his book, *Stick to Your Vision*. I have had the good fortune to work closely with this musical pioneer, to inspire and motivate young people to follow their dreams. His message was always about hope and believing in yourself. I know I speak for thousands when I say his work continues to inspire others worldwide. This multi-talented artist now turns his attention to sharing personal anecdotes and stories to support people in their journey to success, something he knows so well. As Joel Barker said, 'Vision without action is merely a dream. Action without vision passes time. Vision with action can change the world.' Read this book and join Wes's crusade to help you *Stick to Your Vision*."

— Christopher Spence (Director of Education, Toronto District School Board)

"Wes is a monster. Always working, pushing himself, challenging himself to do better, to be better. He's incredibly hard working, tenacious and insatiable in his need to conquer whatever he sets his mind to."

— George F. Walker (Writer/Producer)

"In January 2009, I invited Wes Williams into a facility to speak to incarcerated youth. Being a legendary Canadian hip hop icon, it was easy for him to capture their attention. But more profound than this, Wes spoke from his heart about what it took to overcome the challenges he has faced in his own life, earning the respect of these young men – something not nearly as easy to attain. Wes has a message for young people to rise up, find their vision and believe in themselves – no matter who might doubt them or try to keep them down."
  – Laura Sygrove (Co-founder and Executive Director, New Leaf Yoga Foundation, youth correctional facility)

"When I directed the video for 'Stick to Your Vision,' it reminded me that when we were growing up, Maestro truly represented us all. He really made us feel that we could reach our goals by staying dedicated to whatever we set our minds to."
  – Director X (Music Video Director)

"It's no secret that Wes kicked open an incredibly important door and blazed a trail for not only Canadian 'hip hop' artists, but the Canadian music community as a whole. And yet, in him, you would not find a boastful or arrogant man. Instead, you will encounter a man who possesses humility, gratitude, kindness, authenticity, and a verve that is downright infectious. I feel fortunate to witness such strength of character in a man I not only admire, but am proud to call a friend. When this man speaks – it would be wise to listen. I dare you not to be inspired!"
  – esthero (Singer/Songwriter)

"Wes Williams knows of what he speaks. His wonderful mix of talent, resilience and honesty make him a true role model for young people. Wes, you are my hero. And your forthright book will make you a hero to many more!"
– Linda Schuyler (Creator and Executive Producer, *Instant Star*; Co-Creator and Executive Producer, the *Degrassi* series)

"Canada's music talent of all genres would not know how high to jump without Wes 'Maestro' Williams. There's no measure in Canadian culture to absolutely gauge this compelling hip hop artist and actor forever on the move. So full of music, his staggering command of varied genres places him alongside traditional giants of each while his ability to amalgamate art and popular culture has made him an icon of popular culture alongside the likes of Leonard Cohen, Gordon Lightfoot, and Neil Young. As well, his open-hearted and direct approach to his life continues to touch and inspire so many of us."
– Larry LeBlanc (Senior Writer, *CelebrityAccess/Encore*)

stick to your
VISION

stick to your
VISION

How to Get Past the Hurdles & Haters to Get Where You Want to Be

Wes "Maestro" Williams
With Tamara Hendricks-Williams

McClelland & Stewart

Library and Archives Canada Cataloguing in Publication

Maestro Fresh-Wes
    Stick to your vision : how to get past the hurdles and haters to get where you want to be / Wes "Maestro" Williams with Tamara Hendricks-Williams ; foreword by Chuck D.

ISBN 978-0-7710-8882-7

1. Self-actualization (Psychology). 2. Goal (Psychology).
3. Success. I. Hendricks-Williams, Tamara II. Title.

BF637.S4M332 2010   158.1   C2010-901458-8

We acknowledge the financial support of the Government of Canada through the Book Publishing Industry Development Program and that of the Government of Ontario through the Ontario Media Development Corporation's Ontario Book Initiative. We further acknowledge the support of the Canada Council for the Arts and the Ontario Arts Council for our publishing program.

Published simultaneously in the United States of America by McClelland & Stewart Ltd., P.O. Box 1030, Plattsburgh, New York 12901

Library of Congress Control Number: 2010923467

Typeset in Electra by M&S, Toronto
Printed and bound in the United States of America

This book is printed on paper that is 20% recycled
(20% post-consumer waste).

McClelland & Stewart Ltd.
75 Sherbourne Street
Toronto, Ontario
M5A 2P9
www.mcclelland.com

1 2 3 4 5   14 13 12 11 10

To our son, Chancellor

CONTENTS

Three: DESTINATION

Overleaf: Me and Chuck D taking a break during a hip hop panel in Vancouver. (Photo by David Bernie, 2008)

FOREWORD

Maestro, Sticking to His Vision and Ours

There's a stubborn mountain to scale on the hip hop and rap music terrain, which has driven many an MC or a DJ residing outside of the New York metropolitan area crazy. For the past thirty years of the recorded rap games existence, outsiders of the New York City suburbs of New Jersey, Long Island, Westchester, and Connecticut have had to try harder, be harder, and simply be better to get up that mountain. It has always been this way. The arrogance and ego of the rappers at the peak, arrogance and ego they needed to jump off their genre into the world, set the standard for the competition. This same ego-soaked standard – an attitude of elitism mixed with northeastern swagger – was adopted across rap cities like Philadelphia, Los Angeles, the San Francisco Bay Area, Texas, Chicago, Florida, and Detroit. Eventually it prevailed in all the U.S., and cast its shadow over rappers across the growing hip hop planet.

When I was a kid, my parents often drove upstate, then north of the border through New York, and made an international vacation out of it in Canada. Still, it always seemed to me like we hadn't left Upstate New York, given how close it was. Fifteen years later, as a professional adult, touring with Public Enemy in Canada was a warm reminder of my visits there. I respected that past experience and so I took a special interest in performing in that great growing rap territory on the hip hop planet. I knew and studied the cities there. In 1989 during a U.S. tour, we were in the Midwest and we travelled across the Detroit River to the peaceful city of Windsor. Having family in Detroit, I had been there before and was familiar with the area. We were doing a show at an ice arena and I remember seeing the name Maestro Fresh-Wes on the bill. When I met him after his set, I discovered in person a humble spirit who displayed a Big Daddy Kane wrath on stage.

That night I witnessed a cat who had done his homework, as most Canadian MCs had to do (and continue to do to this day). After all, the Canadian hip hop scene was being shaped by a very dedicated and discerning crowd, from the press and television networks, most notably MuchMusic, to the labels, DJs, and the artists. Maestro was proving to be a versatile blend of what the best MCs were offering at that time, and his interviews were very sharp because they went deeper than the surface of just rap music; they dealt with the whole culture that shaped the hip hop movement.

Maestro has held his own as the king of MCs in Canadian hip hop history. He is the alpha, and he paved the road for other MCs to follow, including the likes of Choclair, Kardinal Offishall, Butta Babies, and the queen of Canadian hip hop, Michie Mee. In hip hop, it is key to not only stay true to the roots of the game but also to stay true to the black-Caribbean culture that has figured so strongly in its energy. Dignity and respect come with that blend, something that is often ignored by American MCs. Canadian MCs never go backward; it's not in their DNA.

Maestro has opened doors not only for rappers, but also for actors, and now for writers, by blazing his own trail and exposing the rich black-Canadian talent that has spawned a nation of super rappers, DJs, graff cats, and breakers. Take the sensational millennial rhymer Drake. I bet my last dollar that he follows the path that Maestro created many years ago and still paves today. Maestro is truly a hip hop god.

Chuck D
Co-founder of classic rap group Public Enemy

PREFACE

Some of you might know me as Maestro Fresh-Wes. Some of you might know me as Wes Williams the actor. Some of you might have no idea who I am but you thought the book cover looked interesting. Doesn't matter. You're reading this now, and for that I thank you.

Here's the deal: I'm a hip hop artist, an actor, and a public speaker from Scarborough, a suburb of Toronto, Canada. I grew up in the 70s when there weren't many black folks on TV or in pop culture. The civil rights movement, the assassinations of Dr. Martin Luther King, Jr., and Malcolm X, those were closer to current events than to history. It was an age of serious transformation about what it meant to be black in Canada and in the world.

The first time I heard a rap song – a record my dad brought home called "Rapper's Delight" by Sugarhill Gang – I knew that's what I wanted to do. Except rap music didn't really exist in Canada. Long story short (the long version is in the rest of this book), I worked my ass off, and between that and good timing, in 1989, when I was twenty-one, my first single, "Let Your Backbone Slide," blew up the Canadian airwaves. It was the first Canadian hip hop track to appear on *Billboard*'s Top 20 Rap Singles chart, and the first one to go gold in Canada. The props and accolades rolled in, but what meant a lot to me was that the Canadian Academy of Recording Arts and Sciences (CARAS) introduced a rap category at the 1991 Juno Awards, based on the success of my music. Finally, hip hop was getting its shine in Canada. That same year, I became the first winner of the first-ever Juno Award for Best Rap Recording.

I was on tour around that time, and the bus driver told me something I'll never forget. He said, "Always carry a baby picture of you in your wallet. That way, when things get tough, you can look at that photo and think of how far you've come."

So I did. I picked a picture of me at age six, wearing an ugly red turtleneck with a fish on it, the kind of photo that we usually hope winds up lost in the bottom of a shoebox somewhere. Trust me, in the years since then I have had many opportunities to look to that photo for inspiration.

Let me go back. Even though my first album, *Symphony in Effect*, went platinum, and I released more albums after that, I never duplicated the same success I had with my single, "Backbone." Nobody ever said as much, but there were times when it was kind of like people were looking at me as if to say, "Didn't you used to be . . . ?" We all used to be something, and we're all on our way to being something else, and there were moments when I just didn't know what that "something else" was.

One of those "moments" was in 1997, when I was living in Brooklyn, New York, trying to reach the American audience the way I'd been able to reach the Canadian one. It was a tough time. Eight years earlier, everybody knew who I was (in Canada, anyway). I had been on stage in front of packed auditoriums of hollering fans, in magazines and all over TV. But eight years is a lifetime in the music industry. Now I was feeling deflated and doubting myself and questioning my vision.

Don't get me wrong, Brooklyn was dope, but America just wasn't feeling me the way I had hoped. I was at a crossroads: Should I keep at it down here in New York? Go home to Toronto? Quit music completely and go back to college like my parents wanted?

One day, I opened the mailbox and found a box set of CDs: *Oh What a Feeling: A Vital Collection of Canadian Music*. My sister had mailed it to me from Toronto. I was honoured to see "Let Your Backbone Slide" on there along with classics from artists like Alanis Morissette, Neil Young, Joni Mitchell, The Band, Bryan Adams, Steppenwolf . . . four CDs of Canada's wealth of musical talent. "Backbone" was sandwiched between Glass Tiger and Bruce Cockburn, which shows you just how humbling it was.

For me, being in this collection meant my industry was acknowledging that I'd done something big. No matter where I was at that moment, or what I'd been through, or what was ahead, I'd always know that I'd made a major contribution to the Canadian music industry. Just the fact that "Backbone" was part of the compilation was huge, because it was *hip hop*.

I put on the CDs, relaxed on my couch, and started to relive my early years through the songs I'd grown up with. Bachman-Turner Overdrive's "Takin' Care of Business," Blood, Sweat and Tears' "Spinning Wheel," Parachute Club's "Rise Up" . . . Now, you can't have an album of Vital Canadian Songs without The Guess Who's song "These Eyes." So when it came on, I felt like a six-year-old again. Man, I used to love that joint as a kid. I heard it all the time.

So I listened to the song and let the memories marinate in my mind.

For some reason, the song made me think of "Backbone." I felt nostalgic and reflected on my life and my career – my beginnings, my first success as an artist. Right then, while listening to "These Eyes," I had an epiphany – I needed to keep it moving, to get back on my journey's path. This decision marked the end of a chapter in my life but also the beginning of a new one. I was leaving the "used to be" and moving into the "going to be."

I got up and began playing "These Eyes" over and over, and then I started writing some lyrics during the eight-bar break:

> *I've seen a lot of valleys, I've seen a lot of peaks,*
> *I've seen the bitter with the sweet, victory and defeat.*
> *Sometimes I fell but a voice kept saying,*
> *"Son, stick to your vision. Peep the composition."*

That voice was God telling me that it was all going to work out and that I'd be all right. It was a sign that I had more hurdles to clear but that I was going to make it to the finish line if I just had faith.

Then I wrote the chorus, sampling Burton Cummings' voice at two different sections.

> [These Eyes] I've seen a lot of shame in the game,
> [These Eyes] I've seen a lot of pain with the fame,
> [These Eyes] I've seen a lot of highs and lows but
> that's just the way life goes.

I came by those lyrics honestly. Fame is a roller-coaster, and it's fickle. Even my own lyrics were telling me it was time to get back to Toronto. Time to get back to my foundation, to the city I love and that helped mould me into the brother I am. I would go back to show everyone that I didn't "used to be" Maestro. I would go back to show them that Maestro was still here, stronger than before because of all the knocks I'd taken.

I recorded that song with the "These Eyes" sample and released it with the title "Stick to Your Vision" on my album *Built to Last* in 1998.

I called it "Stick to Your Vision" because it came out around the ten-year anniversary of my inception as Maestro Fresh-Wes – I had put out my very first Maestro demo tape on college radio back in 1988 – and I was still persevering and sticking to my vision. I knew there was something universal in the experience I was talking about – "I've seen the bitter with the sweet, victory and defeat" – but I had no idea of the impact the song would have. Throughout the years I have heard from countless people – students and artists, musicians, athletes, entrepreneurs – that it inspired them and kept them going. Anyone who had a vision knew what it meant to struggle with achieving it and could relate to my words.

Then, in 2001, I was honoured with a Lifetime Achievement Award at the Urban Music Association of Canada (UMAC) awards. In 2003, I won a Trailblazer Award from the Toronto Reel World Film Festival. Three years later, I was one of the first ten inductees to The Scarborough Walk of Fame. This award especially meant a lot because it demonstrated the support of my community and showed me how I'd been able to make a positive impact on a lot of people's lives. It occurred to me during the Walk of Fame ceremony that maybe I should write a book about my experiences and the lessons I've learned along the way. But I put that idea on the back burner and continued doing my thing (which at the time was music, and making the transition into acting).

Later that same year, 2006, I was on my way to a show in London, Ontario. The cat who drove me (a friend of a friend) was a real laid-back, soft-spoken, mellow dude. He let me know right away that not only was he a true hip hop head, but he was also a big Maestro fan. He started telling me how important my song "Stick to Your Vision" had been to him. Now, like I said earlier, I'd been hearing for years how this song had inspired people, so I was flattered but didn't think much more of it. I thanked him. My man shook his head and said, "Maestro, you really don't understand what I'm saying. That song means *a lot* to me." He rolled up his sleeve, and on his forearm was a tattoo of the words "Stick to Your Vision." Whoa, that was intense. He wanted to live with those words – by those words – for the rest of his life. It was an absolute honour to know that my words affected him so much that he decided to brand them on his skin. That's when I decided I had to put my wheels in motion and write this book.

Look, I'm not a shrink, I'm not a professional life coach, and my only Ph.D. is from the School of Hard Knocks. But what I did worked for me, and this book is just me passing along what I've learned, hoping it will help you. Your challenges are going to have different specifics, but in my experience, the obstacles we all face, when you look at what's underneath them, have a lot of similarities, regardless of whether you're a rapper or a student or a doctor or a painter. Anyone who breaks the mould experiences the same *types* of challenges.

I've been blessed to have some special opportunities to share my experiences with my community. I do motivational speaking for everybody from young kids to adults in community centres to immigrants who have worked their asses off to achieve their dream of becoming new Canadian citizens. Like everybody else, I have had setbacks and disappointments, and by sharing some of them in this book, I hope to give others the strength and will to start their own journeys, to persevere when it gets tough, and to stay optimistic.

Peace and Blessings,
Wes "Maestro" Williams

ACKNOWLEDGEMENTS

First off, I'd like to thank God for blessing me with the gifts and lessons I've learned throughout my life and for the ability to share these in this book. I hope the words on these pages are enlightening and entertaining to the readers.

I'd also like to thank my wife and co-writer, Tamara. You did an excellent job helping me transform these stories into a book and I'm very proud of you. I would not have been able to complete this project without your love, dedication and support.

To my man Chuck D – You are the most prolific voice in the history of hip hop. When I was a kid you signed my T-shirt after a PE concert, and to have you give this project such a powerful endorsement means a lot to me.

To Elizabeth Kribs, my editor at McClelland & Stewart – Thank you for mentoring me through this project. It was a pleasure working with you.

To my friend Terry Markus – You were the one who gave me the phone number to McClelland & Stewart (obviously I put it to good use). Thank you for your continued support.

To Randolph Eustace Walden – Thanks for the early encouragement and guidance in helping me get this thing published.

I'd also like to thank the following for their contributions during the writing and publishing stages of this project: Marilyn Biderman, Sarah Chauncey, Josh Glover, Eric Jensen, Doug Pepper, Susan Renouf, Lynn Schellenberg, Leah Springate, Andrew Roberts, Anna Keenan, David Bernie, Jill Kitchener.

To those who wrote such kind words about me and my work in support of this book, "thank you" doesn't begin to explain how much I appreciate your endorsements: Joel Goldberg, Little X, Adam Rodriguez, Drake, Larry LeBlanc, Esthero, George F. Walker and Dani Romain, Justin Bua, Chris Spence, Laura Sygrove, George Stroumboulopoulos and Linda Schuyler.

To my family: Mom, Dad, Warren, Mel Boogie, Dexter, Xavier, Kianna, and Darius. The Williams and the Matthews families, the Hendricks and Grew families. Rich London and family.

To all the people who have supported me along the path to *my vision:* All my friends and colleagues in the music, film and television industries. To all my fans – thanks for the love.

INTRODUCTION: **HOW TO USE THIS BOOK**

I f you have a vision of what you want for your life and who you want to be, this book will show you how to deal with some of the obstacles in your way (and you might be surprised where they come from). If you haven't discovered your purpose, or you're at a crossroads like I was back in 1997 (check out the Preface for the whole story), there are some exercises that will help you define your vision. I hope to inspire and encourage anyone who is working towards a destination.

This book has three main sections; each one is kicked off with an anecdote called Talkin' Windows. This three-part story is a metaphor for the choices you have to make about your vision for your life.

The first section, "**Expectation**," deals with preconceived notions that others have placed on us and that we in turn have placed on ourselves about what we can and cannot do. The chapters in this section talk about the importance of breaking these barriers and establishing your own terms. This section is where I discuss clarifying or defining your vision.

"**Operation**," the second section, explores putting your plan into action. Once you have pinpointed your purpose, it's time to map out how to fulfill it. This section's chapters describe helpful tools and the ways in which you can create the ideal conditions to achieve your vision.

The third section, "**Destination**," is about what you can do once you accomplish your goals. These final chapters deal with everything from celebrating your victories to helping others and creating new goals for yourself.

You'll notice different features throughout the book. There are sidebars, which I've titled "BTW." These are like my side thoughts, as if I'm saying to you "by the way." They're extra things I wanted to mention and sometimes they even take a different point of view. I've included these to start a dialogue, to get (and keep) you thinking.

I also wanted to share sayings and quotes that I've found uplifting. There's a lot of positive energy out there and I take inspiration from wherever I can get it. These words come from many different people – musicians, actors, athletes, writers, motivational leaders and visionary thinkers, both past and present. I've picked one quote to kick off each section and chapter, and I hope they inspire you too.

As well, in the "Operation" section of the book, I've added "Shoutouts" to some people who have inspired me at different points in my life and career. These features provide some more detail on how these individuals' own challenges and accomplishments have encouraged me.

I've included different exercises to help you along, sort of like a guide. These are meant to help you transform your thoughts into something tangible. Some of the exercises can be completed inside this book, in the spaces provided, but I also recommend you get yourself a notebook or a binder with loose-leaf paper, and start your own Vision Book. Your Vision Book is for your eyes only and I encourage you to add to it even after you're finished reading *Stick to Your Vision*.

But the thing is, anyone can do these exercises using only half their brainpower. It is the fire within you – your passion and desire – that makes all the difference. You're reading this book, so you're obviously in tune with that voice inside of you to some degree. You need to tap into it, learn to channel that voice, so that you can use it as a compass to keep you on the right track. If you train yourself to quiet all the idle chit-chat, whether it's running through your brain or out of your homie's mouth, you'll be able to hear what your inner voice is telling you. Let that voice guide you through the exercises.

You will see <<REWIND near the end of each chapter, before the exercise. When I read, I like to underline points that hit me in the head, that really stand out to me, but I can't tell you what to do with these jewels. So I have reiterated these points at the end of each chapter – just look for the <<REWIND symbol. If you're in a rush and don't have time to read the whole chapter but are in desperate need of some

quick tips, you can flip to the end of the chapter and read the <<REWIND first. Then go back and read the rest of the chapter when you have more time.

One more thing – know that, even though this book has a last page, I'm not finished. Not by a long shot. I'm right there with you, still on my own journey, taking it day by day.

We owe it to ourselves to believe in our vision, to keep positive energy around us as we focus on reaching our goals. We have to believe in ourselves. Just keep it moving.

STICK TO YOUR VISION

Yo, brothers ain't seen what I seen in this game son
Been in this game a long, long, long time
Still strivin' though
Yo, ninety-nine
It's the visine baby, it's the visine
Yo

I've built with Israelites, Rastafarians, God bodies
F.O.I., Sunni Muslims, T.O. to Brooklyn
Many nights in Bed-Stuy, blazin' trees out in Cali
With brothers from frat, sippin' Henny, mad friendly
Got Toronto's rap title, done mad recitals
Met Quincy Jones in eighty-nine, that's my idol
Chicks from every nationality, showin' hospitality
Grabbin' me, showin' mad love in the club
Peep the style, listen, check my rendition
Performed for royalty and politicians
Even done shows with the greatest MCs of all time
I was the one who used to say "eighty-nine is mine"
I've seen a lot of valleys, I've seen a lot of peaks
I've seen the bitter with the sweet, victory and defeat
Sometimes I fell, but a voice kept saying
Son, stick to your vision, peep the composition

[Chorus]
[These Eyes] I've seen a lot of shame in the game
[These Eyes] I've seen a lot of pain with the fame
[These Eyes] I've seen a lot of highs and lows, but
that's just the way life goes
[These Eyes] I've seen my name written in lights
[These Eyes] I've seen a lot of things in my life
[These Eyes] I've seen a lot of highs and lows, but
that's just the way life goes

I grab the microphone, like the priest does a rosary
Jehova be shinin' when clouds are over me
So I recollect, remember Kid Capri
On 'BLS played my joint when I heard "Protect Ya
Neck"
Back in ninety-two, but let's go back to eighty-eight
Flemingdon, Don Mills and Eglinton
Makin' beats with S and Jel and them
Remember when you labels wasn't feelin' me
Next year changed the scenery, gave birth to your
energy
Toured with Ice-T and Public Enemy
MUCH gave me love, you n— had to envy me
Couldn't stand to see a brother shine
Player haters always workin' overtime (I ain't blind)
I've seen a lot of valleys, I've seen a lot of peaks

I've seen the bitter with the sweet, victory and defeat
Sometimes I fell, but a voice kept sayin'
Son, stick to your vision, peep the composition

[Chorus]

Yo, people used to say Wes, wake up, stop dreamin'
You fantasize, fuck the rappin', it won't happen
I paid my dues, brothers seen me sacrifice
Another song in the key of life
Mr. Maes got the iller track, I did a three sixty
Seen God starin' in the mirror, black
I figured that if I stayed focused, when situations
    seemed hopeless
I'm elevatin', breakin' the spell of Satan
I want my lyrics written out like Esco
To show the rap world how the industry slept
So when I'm gone, the parable will carry on
Young cats can sit back, puff trom, cool out, and
    sing along
I've seen a lot of valleys, I've seen a lot of peaks
I've seen the bitter with the sweet, victory and defeat
Sometimes I fell, but a voice kept sayin'
Son, stick to your vision, stick to your vision
I've seen a lot of valleys, I've seen a lot of peaks
I've seen the bitter with the sweet, victory and defeat
Sometimes I fell, but a voice kept sayin'
Son, stick to your vision, out

ONE: **EXPECTATION**

"Life's challenges are not supposed to
paralyze you; they're supposed to help you
discover who you are."

– BERNICE JOHNSON REAGON

Overleaf: Hanging out at my man Ebony MC's house. We were practising for a big show. (Photo by Marlon Bruce, Scarborough, 1985)

TALKIN' WINDOWS: PART ONE

We've all heard the phrase "window of opportunity," right? Well, for fun, let's just say there are three windows and they can talk. How would that go down? The first window is wide open and it talks in a loud but appealing voice. It's telling you to come inside. You take a look at it and say to yourself, "I know I can get through this window because it's totally open, but let me go check the second window before I commit."

You then proceed to the second window, which is half open, or half closed, depending on how you look at it. This window starts talking to you too. Its voice is not as loud as the first window but it's still fairly appealing to you. You take a look at the window and say to yourself, "I can still get through this. It's half open (or half closed) but with little to no effort I can still slide through. I know I can get through both Window Number One and Window Number Two, but let me check out what Window Number Three is saying."

You head over to the third window and see it's practically closed shut. So you say to yourself, "Screw it, this is gonna take some work to open, so let me just go back and check out the other two windows."

As you start to walk back to the previous windows, you hear a loud voice coming from Window Number Three. It begins speaking to you.

WINDOW NUMBER THREE:
Where are you going? You're really gonna check those two clowns? C'mon, son. Tell me you're kidding.

YOU:
Are you talking to me?

WINDOW NUMBER THREE:
No, I'm talking to that door over there. Of course I'm talking to you. Don't ask stupid questions. Do you know what those two jokers are really about?

YOU:
No, but I'm sure you'll tell me . . .

WINDOW NUMBER THREE:
Look, there's no need for sarcasm. I'm trying to help you out.

YOU:
Okay, I'm sorry. Tell me about those two windows.

WINDOW NUMBER THREE:

Now, first of all, why do you think Window Number One is open like that, huh? He's got the loudest mouth on the whole block. Talking loud but saying nothin'! He's known around here as The Window of Complacency. Yeah, you could mess with him but trust me, my man, you won't be happy in the end. Any Tom, Dick, or Harry can go through that window. There's no effort needed at all.

YOU:

I see. So what's up with the second window?

WINDOW NUMBER THREE:

He's known on the streets as The Window of Mediocrity. He's not as wack as Complacency but he still won't give you what you're looking for. If you're truly ready to see what you're made of you should be dealing with me. You gotta work to get through but I know you can do it. You just need to raise your expectations of yourself.

To be continued…

I: **BLACK MEN CAN'T SKATE**

"Reexamine all that you have been told in school, or in church or in any book. Dismiss whatever insults your soul."

— WALT WHITMAN

I was six years old the first time I heard the "N word." I was the only black kid in my first grade class of twenty. There was an East Indian girl, but the other eighteen kids were white.

The teacher asked each of us to draw a picture of what we wanted to be when we grew up (you remember those assignments, right?). She left us alone with our crayons, and we all began drawing.

I wanted to be #4, Bobby Orr, the Wayne Gretzky of the time. So I carefully drew him in the black-and-gold Boston Bruins jersey instead of the stupid red turtleneck with a fish on it that I was sporting. I used my brown Crayola to make him black, and the black one to give him an Afro. Keep in mind this is long before the NHL had black superstars like Jarome Iginla.

I was looking at my picture, pretty proud of it, when this blond kid checked out my drawing, looked at me, and said, "You can't play hockey. You're a nigger."

Then he swung at me.

Before I knew it, he and seven other boys were piling on me and beating the hell out of me for having the audacity to want to be a hockey player – a black hockey player. I remember thinking I was going to throw up after one kid punched me in the stomach. I saw the East Indian girl looking at me, and she had this expression on her face as if to say "Wish I could help you out, buddy, but you're on your own." She knew the deal.

BTW: Black Men in the NHL

When I was a kid, the idea of a black man playing professional hockey – well, you know the story. Brothers were supposed to play basketball, supposed to play football, supposed to box. That was society's expectation.

I obviously wasn't the only black kid who wanted to be a pro hockey player. Jarome Iginla, all-star and captain of the Calgary Flames (and a much younger cat than I am) has said that when kids told him he didn't "look like" an NHL player, he took inspiration from goalie Grant Fuhr, who played in the league for almost two decades, including the Gretzky Stanley Cup–winning era of the Edmonton Oilers.

That's why I'm so proud to see brothers like Jarome among the NHL's most respected players, continuing to pave the way. Someday, nobody will tell the next Iggy he doesn't "look like" an NHL star.

And I learned it too that day. The deal was that these kids saw me as "less than" them, because I looked different. That day I learned that people put expectations on you – high or low – based on superficial things. I was beaten up because of my skin colour, but I'm sure there were other kids who were bullied or teased for other reasons. "Too short," "too tall," "too fat," "too smart," "too dumb," from the "wrong" neighbourhood – if you didn't fit into this box they expected you to stay in, they were going to try and shove you back in your "place." It didn't matter what you wanted to do or *could* do.

Growing up, my family lived in an apartment in the North York area of Toronto. I used to play with our next-door neighbours, a young girl and her brother. One day, she looked at me and said, "Wes, when are you going to turn white?" Like my skin was going to change along with my height, and maybe I was just a little slow developing.

With my six-year-old logic, I actually thought that was a pretty good question. So after dinner one night, I turned to my dad and asked, "Dad, when am I going to turn white?" My dad chuckled and said in his Guyanese accent, "Boy, I'm still waiting."

People put expectations on you – high or low – based on superficial things.

Looking back, I think he handled that the right way – with humour.

I'm telling you all this because it illustrates what I was up against. It was difficult to figure out where I fit in; I was ostracized because I wasn't like everyone else.

You know, sometimes people's expectations of you don't always come out in a negative way, like being bum-rushed by a bunch of bullies. Expectations like those aren't hard to figure out. Sometimes it's the subtle ones that can hurt more.

My little neighbour was asking me an innocent question, but I guess I had already figured out that "white was right" or I would've asked her when she was turning black 'cause "black's where it's at." I suppose most of us learn quite early in our lives that majority rules. Since then, I have learned, and I hope you will also, that sometimes when you're sticking to your vision, you're going against the majority.

<<REWIND

People put expectations on you based on what they've been taught. If you're different than they are, and you want to do something that isn't in their realm of imagination, they may try to stop you or try to put you "back in your place," verbally or physically. Identifying these expectations is the first step to overcoming them.

Exercise I: **Identifying Your Assumptions**

This is a good time to begin your Vision Book, which is your personal journal to record your thoughts, feelings, and progress towards your vision. You can get an inexpensive one from your local dollar store or a fancy one from a stationery store, whatever works for you and makes it yours. Some of the exercises in this book have blank spaces where you can answer the questions but you might need more space or prefer to record your thoughts in your personal Vision Book.

1. Write down three limiting assumptions people have made about you. Who made them, and what did they give as a reason (if any)?

_____

_____

_____

_____

_____

_____

2. The people who said these things, why do you think – in terms of their lives, their backgrounds – they put that on you?

_____

_____

_____

_____

3. How have those assumptions affected you in
   terms of what you want to do? What you think
   you can do? What you think you can't do?

_____

_____

_____

_____

4. Who inspires you? If you can't think of someone,
   list the qualities in others you find inspiring.

_____

_____

_____

_____

2: DEFINING EXPECTATIONS OF YOURSELF

"I will not let you walk through my mind
with your dirty feet."

— MAHATMA GANDHI

We learn to define ourselves, and our expectations of ourselves, based on other's expectations of us – which, often, we pick up from the people around us and the media. Once you understand how other people's experiences have affected their expectations of you – and, in some cases, what their motives are – you can learn to disregard the harmful or unproductive ones and come up with your own expectations.

We all play a variety of different roles in our lives – in our families, society, relationships, school, and elsewhere. Each of these situations puts expectations on us, whether high or low. If you get good grades you might be expected to become a lawyer, not a painter. If your grades aren't so good, you might be expected to work in the trades, and not in medicine.

Everyone has a different "story." Your "story" is everything everybody (including you) has ever told you about yourself to this point in your life. It's your ethnicity, it's where you grew up, it's what your teachers told you that you could and couldn't do, it's your religion, it's what you excel in, it's what you're not so good at. Your story is your idea of who you think, and who you've been told, you are.

But regardless of who you are, whatever your vision is, you've got to be in an environment that reflects your experience without judgment.

As we grow up, we need people who say "I feel you" and who reinforce the individual identity we're trying to develop – people who accept us. We need to feel that we are part of a community that reflects and reinforces our identity and experiences. We also need to know where we come from, the context of our lives. People who are part of the majority tend to take for granted all the mirrors around them. Those in the minority, however, will most definitely notice the lack of reflections around them. If, everywhere you look, there's nobody who resembles you or comes from where you come from, you might feel invalidated, like an outcast.

> Your "story" is everything everybody (including you) has ever told you about yourself to this point in your life.

My Story

My story begins in Canada, where I was born. When I was five months old, my parents sent me to live with my grandparents in Guyana, South America, and I was with them until I moved back to Canada to be with my parents at the age of four. After moving back to Canada, I remember the first face I saw on TV that looked like mine was Muhammad Ali. He was in the prime of his fighting career, standing there chanting "Quarry! Quarry!" provoking his opponent Jerry Quarry. And I wanted to be there with him. I asked my mom, "Mommy, can I jump in the TV?" That's how I'd get to talk to Muhammad Ali. He looked like *me*. I felt an instant connection to him, because he had the same skin colour I did.

This was the first time I saw a black man on TV; it was also one of the only positive images of a black man on TV at that time.

Growing up in Toronto in the 1970s, my story was that I was different from everyone else because of my race. That also meant I didn't have a lot of role models in the media. Canada's hit TV shows at the time were *The Beachcombers* and *King of Kensington*. I couldn't relate to them; they didn't have any black folks. Instead, I watched the African-American shows on American TV, sitcoms like *The Jeffersons, Good Times*, and *What's Happening!!* I loved waking up Saturday mornings to watch joints like *Fat Albert and the Cosby Kids* or *The Harlem Globetrotters Popcorn Machine*. Here were characters I could identify with, even though they were mostly just light entertainment. It was as if you could be black on TV as long as you were a joker, as long as you were funny. Those were the expectations, the unspoken rules. Still, as a young cat growing up, that's all I saw, and I felt comfortable watching these shows, because their characters "looked" like me.

Then I entered a new chapter in my life.

Roots

In the summer of 1977, I was blown away by the miniseries *Roots*. In case you haven't heard of it, *Roots* is the story of African-American author Alex Haley's family tree: how his ancestors were kidnapped from Gambia, a country in West Africa, and taken to America as part of the slave trade, where they were stripped of their names, religion, and culture. I don't think there had ever been anything like that on TV.

It was a groundbreaking moment in the history of television – having a show about black people on prime time for six nights in a row. And the characters weren't court jesters; they didn't have to be goofy. I learned where people who looked like me came from. (I don't know about other schools, but mine sure didn't teach any kind of black history. So this was my first lesson.) Finally, I felt acknowledged.

For six nights, I sat on the couch, glued to our twenty-seven-inch Zenith TV. Six straight nights of black people on TV. Discovering: *there's a whole continent of people who look like me.*

I was only nine so I didn't really have an intellectual reaction to what I was viewing or to the idea of racism, because I was just trying to understand what it meant to be black – what it meant to be me. I was just learning what it meant to be called the N word, what it meant that, before *Roots*, the only black people I'd seen on TV were comic stereotypes, and just learning why these white men changed Kunta Kinte's name, why they were whipping him. Kunta Kinte had tried to run, so the slave masters cut off his foot, so he couldn't run. Watching *Roots* showed me how black people had been abused and stripped of their identity and why I indirectly had a hard time being accepted.

I saw the importance of knowing my history although I couldn't fully understand it at the time. Before *Roots*, I didn't know that my last name, Williams, was a slave master's name, and that I had been robbed of my original name. At the time I had no idea that it was by design that I didn't have any role models or examples around me – I wasn't *supposed* to figure out who I was.

Rapper's Delight

One of the biggest revelations in my story occurred a couple of years later. My dad was a huge music fan, and he was always playing records by artists like Bob Marley and other reggae, soca, funk, jazz – a lot of jazz, like Miles Davis, Duke Ellington, Thelonious Monk, and Count Basie – and soul, like Marvin Gaye and Stevie Wonder. One night in 1979, my dad brought home this record called "Rapper's Delight" by Sugarhill Gang. I was eleven and it changed my life. "Rapper's Delight" was very similar to Chic's hit "Good Times," except, instead of singing, these guys were rhyming over the rhythm. The flow of their rhymes and the lyrics were dope!

Beats and rhymes. What a fly combination! I knew that somehow, some day, I wanted to be a part of this. I began listening to all the rap I could find, and tracks like "The Breaks" by Kurtis Blow, "Super Rhymes" by Jimmy Spicer, and Grandmaster Flash's "The Message" just got me more hooked. I was going to be a rapper.

At that age, I wasn't thinking about making a living rapping, much less dreaming the superstar dream of record contracts, mansions, fast cars – even women – not really. The music sounded cool, that's why I wanted to try to do it. When I messed around with it a little and tried to rhyme over the instrumental versions of the records, I found I was good at it. My flow needed some work but my lyrics were dope – I could do this! Of course, the fact that the girls appreciated my skills made it even more exciting. I was hooked on hip hop and there was no turning back.

<<REWIND

Knowing your story is essential to understanding yourself and your aspirations, because your story helps you identify the expectations placed on you – which, in turn, define the challenges you'll face.

Exercise 2: **Writing Your Story**

1. Use the space provided below, or a page in your Vision Book, to write your story.

_____

_____

_____

_____

_____

_____

_____

_____

_____

_____

_____

_____

_____

2. What expectations or limitations have been put on you based on your story?

_____

_____

a) What are the roles you play that make you feel deflated, discouraged, and fake?

_____

_____

b) What are the roles you play that make you feel energized, amped, and authentic?

_____

_____

3. Are you living in your ideal environment?

_____

_____

a) Does such a place exist or can you find some of the things you need where you are now?

_____

_____

b) Do you need to relocate?

_____

_____

3: DEFYING EXPECTATIONS

*"Making your mark on the world is hard. If
it were easy, everybody would do it. But it's
not. It takes patience, it takes commitment,
and it comes with plenty of failure along
the way. The real test is not whether you
avoid this failure, because you won't. It's
whether you let it harden or shame you
into inaction, or whether you learn from it;
whether you choose to persevere."*

— BARACK OBAMA

For most of high school I attended Senator
O'Connor, a Catholic school with only about
twelve hundred students. Though it didn't have
many black students, it was still ethnically diverse
enough that I didn't feel like a pepper-grain in a salt-
factory. We had to wear uniforms but we were allowed
to make some cool alterations, kind of like Will Smith's
character in *The Fresh Prince of Bel-Air*. Baggie pants

and Chinese slippers were hot in 1982 and 1983, so that's how I'd rock my uniform.

I got more involved in rap in high school, too. And as fate would have it, this is also where I met the brothers Peter and Anthony Davis, known as First Offence, who would later end up producing my first album, *Symphony in Effect.* I adopted the name Melody MC and performed at high school dances. One night, after a wicked show, my friend Joey Lecachi told me he could get me on radio. Radio! I could get my rhymes to a lot more people than I could at dances.

I was fifteen, and my only frame of reference for the inside of a radio station was from the sitcom *WKRP in Cincinnati.* I was thinking Venus Flytrap, Herb with the wack pants . . . But Joey was talking about college radio, CKLN at Ryerson University (coincidentally, the same place my dad got his engineering degree). It had the only rap show in Toronto, *The Fantastic Voyage*, which aired every Saturday afternoon.

The building was a maze. On my way to the "studio," I got lost in almost every wing of that place, maybe some twice. Finally we found the door that said CKLN. To say I was excited was an understatement; I felt like an all-star.

This wasn't WKRP, which was cool – I just wanted to do my thing. I opened the door and stepped into a tiny little room, very plain and modest.

There were loose papers everywhere – on desks, on the floor – but the thing that really caught my eye was over to the left: the sound booth. I was nervous and excited at the same time, and my heart was pounding.

The host of the show, Ron Nelson, came over to me and introduced himself. He had an Afro and was wearing a burgundy dress shirt, which I guess was kind of like Venus Flytrap.

It was one of those moments you look back on later, because it turns out to be bigger than you thought. Ron Nelson would go on to be one of my biggest motivators. He was a true rap pioneer, one of the most important individuals in the evolution of Canadian hip hop. In addition to hosting *The Fantastic Voyage*, as a concert promoter, Ron brought all the big names to Toronto – everyone from Run-D.M.C., to Boogie Down Productions, to Big Daddy Kane, you name it. In my mind he is the true Godfather of Canadian hip hop.

From the time we met, Ron never fronted on me. I was just a kid, but he always treated me like a peer. He led me to the sound booth, and for a minute, everything felt kind of unreal; it felt like everything was moving in slow motion. I put on the headphones he gave me. I was mad nervous, so I did what I always did. I thought, "How would Michael Jackson handle this?" (R.I.P. He will always be the king.) And I pretended I *was* Michael Jackson, it was like I became him so I could have his confidence, have all the love in the world from the fans. I took a deep breath, and over Vaughn Mason and Crew's instrumental to "Bounce, Rock, Skate, Roll," I kicked my first radio rhyme: "It's Melody Man and I'm back to rhyme / with a brand new rap for a brand new time / And I'm guaranteed to make your body work / 'cause I'll make you people go berserk."

I kept going but it seemed like that's all I rhymed and it was over – that's how fast it felt. Just a blur, and then Ron was shaking my hand as I left the studio. As I was on my way out I recall Ron saying live on-air, "That was Melody MC from Scarborough. He's only fifteen and, damn, he's good!"

After I heard that I *really* felt like an all-star and walked with my chest out. I was very proud of myself.

Most successful people can point to at least one person in their lives who gave them the confidence to go for their dreams. Even though I was already rapping on my own, getting props from Ron – a serious hip hop authority – inspired me to work harder, get better. It was a huge ego boost.

That was the push I needed for my career to really take off. I became a regular guest on *The Fantastic Voyage* for the next couple of years. I owe a lot of thanks, and much respect, to Ron for his support.

Thanks to radio exposure and word of mouth, over the next couple of years, my popularity was growing and I was in high demand at local community centres, dances, and rap battles. I was evolving into a hip hop beast . . . a hip hop beast who was about to start his freshman year at Carleton University, in Ottawa, Canada.

I was doing what I was *supposed* to do. You're *supposed* to graduate high school and you're *supposed* to go to university. That's what I was told, so that's what I did. I had no idea what I wanted to major in, because hip hop wasn't in the curriculum, so I just took law, political science, sociology – I was happy to take anything except math and science! I was so busy with school and my part-time job at Leon's Furniture Warehouse that rap took a backseat.

During the winter semester, I was watching a show on MuchMusic (Canada's equivalent to MTV) called *Soul in the City,* and I saw a local female MC by the name of Michie Mee performing at the Concert Hall, which at the time was the biggest venue for hip hop acts in Toronto. She was introduced by one of the greatest MCs of all time, KRS-One – the co-founder of Boogie Down Productions. To see somebody like him, KRS-One, supporting Michie, a Canadian MC, was both inspiring and a symbol of hope for the future of Canadian hip hop.

That was my turning point. I thought, "Wow, look at her! I remember her from back in the day and she's still doing it. I can't stop. I have to keep doing my thing." So I decided to take a year off university and give my music a real shot.

Well . . . this didn't go over too well with my mom. At first, I didn't tell her I was leaving school to be a rapper. I said I was taking time off to work. After a few months, she caught on, and man, was she pissed. She just wasn't feeling my decision and she didn't hide that fact.

She was angry because she was disappointed. My parents emigrated from Guyana to Canada to provide more opportunities for their family than they'd had. They wanted their children to get a good education and work a white-collar job. They didn't know about the concept of creating a career outside of the box. My father worked for CN Rail in the 1970s and my mom worked at Bell Canada, the phone company, where she stayed until her retirement thirty years later. She didn't have the opportunities to do the things she wanted to do in life. Oddly enough, she's the one who introduced me to music. She played the piano, and she even enrolled me and my siblings in music lessons. To have sacrificed so much to give her first child options, and in her mind, to have me throw those options away, that really broke her heart. She thought I was setting a bad example for my younger brother and sister and that I was wasting my time. Even when I got my record deal, she was upset that I wasn't doing what she thought I should be doing. All she knew was the world she came from, and in that world, education is essential. Being a professional musician wasn't even on her radar. That was something that other people did, and she thought I didn't care about the sacrifices she and my dad had made.

Your loved ones can be jealous of you – and that can include your parents.

I wasn't angry with her. I felt rejected, and it was hard on me not to have her support. I saw where she was coming from but, especially because she inspired me to love music, her reaction was difficult to take. I sometimes wonder whether she might have gone into a music-related field herself if circumstances had been different.

Sometimes parents want their children to accomplish the things they didn't, and they put too much pressure on their kids. Some parents try to live vicariously through their kids, pushing them towards areas that interest the parent more than the child.

On the flip side, your loved ones can be jealous of you – and that can include your parents too. If they didn't have the opportunity to accomplish their dreams or didn't have the luxury to venture off and find themselves, they may be resentful. They may not even know where this feeling comes from.

Just know that if you attempt to please others by doing what they think you're *supposed* to do, you will probably end up feeling like you robbed yourself because you've gone off course from your vision. As bad as it feels to disappoint others, even your parents, it feels even worse to disappoint yourself.

<<REWIND

Not everybody is going to support you in pursuing your dream. Know that when people resist or are negative, it's more likely to be about their own unfulfilled dreams than about you. If you can understand where they're coming from, you'll be able to see it's not personal. It might still bug you, but it won't sting as much.

Exercise 3: **Separating Your Expectations from Others'**

1. When people try to stop you from pursuing your vision, try to figure out where they're coming from. What is *their* story? Why do they have these convictions? Once you figure these things out, you will be able to take their reactions less personally, because you will see that how they're reacting really says more about them than you.

2. Use the table opposite to list the things others expect you to do and then what you expect of yourself. Write down the action you would need to take to fulfill these expectations, and all the positive things that would come with these actions. Then write down the emotions you think you would feel in making these moves.

   Now compare the two halves of the table – which half evokes the most emotion? Which words in the feeling/outcome column speak the most to your personal values? Evaluate the answers to the questions and decide for yourself which side fits in best with your vision of what you want for your life.

WHAT OTHERS EXPECT OF YOU	
Action involved	**Feeling/Outcome**

WHAT YOU EXPECT OF YOURSELF	
Action involved	**Feeling/Outcome**

4: SELF-DEFEATING EXPECTATIONS

"The battles that count aren't the ones for
gold medals. The struggles within yourself –
the invisible, inevitable battles inside all of
us – that's where it's at."

— Jesse Owens

Sometimes we count ourselves out before we even start. Sometimes we think by stopping before the race has even begun that we're sparing ourselves heartache and time, but actually, we're robbing ourselves of the valuable lessons learned from striving for greatness: how to solve problems, be resourceful, heal, hurdle obstacles, think critically, and be confident, resilient, and patient. And there are countless others.

Many times, it's because we're afraid to fail. If you put yourself out there, you're vulnerable. Being vulnerable is scary, so most people play it safe and end up settling for the easiest thing to do instead of the most satisfying.

If we come from an environment in which all our family and friends have stayed within the confines of their expectations, we may start to think it's acceptable to coast – after all, nobody expected us to reach those higher goals anyway.

The same thing can work in reverse, in a family of overachievers; kids may be pushed in academic or professional directions they might not want to go.

It is so important to realize that it's *your* life you have to lead and not anyone else's. Throughout your life, the people around you will be impressed as well as disappointed by the decisions you make, but you are the one who has to figure out your own destination.

My Challenge

I remember in 1988 when I was shopping my demo tapes to record companies in the hope of landing a deal. Everybody, including members of my family, told me I was dreaming. Since no MC in my city had ever had a hit record they assumed it would be impossible. I like to call this type of thinking "The Small Tank Syndrome."

You've probably heard that goldfish grow as big as their environment will allow. That's a myth, but it is true that being in too small a tank will stunt their growth. Same goes for people.

Fortunately, as humans, we don't have to wait for someone else to move us to a bigger tank: we can do it ourselves. It's tough, though, because every time you move to a bigger tank, the sharks (your enemies) get bigger, and hungrier, too. So you have to keep afloat –

keep your eye on your vision and your faith in yourself. Disappointing your people is one thing, but disappointing yourself is much harder to live with.

My whole life, even though others have doubted and underestimated me, I've had extremely high expectations of myself. It's these high expectations that helped me keep going because they gave me something to focus on, which indirectly allowed me to ignore all the naysayers. The way I see it, you have two choices: be focused or be distracted. Some people might call it optimism or pessimism, negativity or positivity. Call it what you want, but just know that it's a choice *you* make. So like I was saying, I focus on the high expectations I've set for myself. But I'm human and sometimes I do lose focus and get blindsided. And I've noticed it's at these times that I slip up. Losing my focus throws me off my game and I walk around like a chicken with my head cut off. I can't find my keys or I'll lock them in my car, my cellphone battery will die and leave me hanging, I'll bomb an audition or I'll stub my toe. You know those times – when anything that can go wrong does. Well, that's what happens to me whenever I lose focus and allow my **It's your life you have to live, not anyone else's.** mind to wander through the lost land of "can't" and "shouldn't." So I take these mishaps as signs to get back on the right track, and I redirect my thoughts to my vision and the steps I need to take to get there. Trust me, this is a lot easier said than done, but it's possible and very necessary.

Some people have internalized the low expectations of society or of their family or friends. They think they are unworthy of success and incapable of achieving it. Because they don't think they'll succeed, they don't even try, and that really bugs me because they're selling themselves short. Going for it means being vulnerable. Being vulnerable means you might get hurt, and that's a thought that paralyzes a lot of people. So they play it safe. It's easier to just coast along under the radar. They might not be living their vision, but by their thinking, at least they're not putting themselves in danger.

And then there are those people who take their low expectations and try to force them on everyone around them. Misery loves company and they figure if they're not going anywhere (or at least not to their desired destination) no one else should either.

"Crabs in a Bucket"

If you're a Canadian hip hop head like me, you probably thought of the k-os song when you saw this heading. But if you've spent time on the shore, you might have seen the literal "crabs in a bucket" phenomenon. When fishermen are gathering crabs from the water, they throw them in a bucket. Naturally, at least one determined crab will try to escape and get back into the water (crabs know what's up). For some reason, the other crabs will try to hold him back.

Imagine one little blue crab trying to climb out of the bucket – he has dreams of getting back to the water instead of being served up for dinner. The minute he

BTW: Nicely Dressed Crabs in a Bucket

It's one thing to internalize other people's low expectations of you — that's something you have to resolve yourself. It's a much bigger problem when members of a visible minority start putting those negative expectations on each other. You're not just hurting yourself; you're hurting your community.

As recently as 2009, there was an occurance that reinforced to me how much some black folks may still have internalized assumptions about each other. I was sitting in a hotel lounge, preparing for a public speaking engagement the next day. There I was, with my espresso in front of me, looking at my notes, answering the various calls that came in on my cellphones (I had two different numbers, one for Toronto, where I am from and frequently travel for work, and one for Vancouver, where I lived at the time).

Two black guys in business suits came up to me. One was in his twenties and the other was in his early thirties. They told me they were from Montreal and were in town for a personal development conference. We chopped it up for a while and we got to know each other.

The younger cat was a fan of mine, and that was cool — he was amped just to see me. I noticed the other one looking at my notes. He said, "You know, man, when I met you, all I knew was that you were a rapper. I saw your two cellphones, your hat turned sideways, and to be honest, what went through my mind was, 'Is he a gangsta for real?' I never would have thought you were preparing a motivational speech."

Even though this dude was enlightened enough to travel a thousand miles to a motivational seminar, he still made assumptions about another brother based on stereotypes.

As important as it is not to let other people's expectations of you define who you are, it's also really important not to put expectations on other people.

starts to climb the side of the bucket, the other crabs start going, "I don't think so," and they gang up on ambitious Lil Blue, dragging him down limb by limb by limb by . . . well, you get the point.

"Crabs in a bucket" has become a phrase used to describe a group of people who would rather hurt one of their own than see him or her escape from their shared environment or circumstances.

With friends like that, who needs haters!?

Subconscious Sabotaging

Some people create what is referred to as a "self-fulfilling prophecy." If you don't believe you can succeed at something or deserve something good, either you won't try or you'll subconsciously sabotage yourself and fail. Then you'll tell yourself, "I should've listened to my family/friends/society. I'm wack at this. I'm a failure." This happens a lot with people who have internal conflicts about going against the advice of people close to them. In order to realize your vision, you have to believe it *is* possible, and you have to believe that you *can* do it. Nobody else can do that for you. You've got to know that when people doubt you or criticize you for sticking to your vision, it might be that they feel threatened or jealous. Most people are afraid to go for what they want. So when you step outside the box, they begin questioning whether they made the right choice by playing it safe. One way they can reconcile this internal conflict is by putting you down and convincing themselves they were right never to stick their necks out in the first place. I don't think people intentionally do this; it's more of a subconscious thing.

Remember, no matter how hard you try, you're not going to make everyone happy. You have to keep in mind that their reactions are about them, not about you. You have to figure out your own destination and the path you're going to take to get there.

I learned this lesson early in my music career. After the triumph of my first album, *Symphony in Effect*, there was pressure to achieve the same success with my sophomore release. So when I recorded *The Black Tie Affair*, everyone had an opinion about it. Needless to say, some people loved it and some people hated it. I had busted my ass and tried to create something that everyone would appreciate. I put party records on there, threw in some West Indian flavour, and I came hard with the lyrics. But then people said they didn't like my flows, or the lyrics weren't dope enough, or whatever. All I know is that I stressed and put so much into it and tried so hard to reach everyone, and people still hated on it. Even though a lot of people loved it, it was really easy to be overwhelmed by the negativity others were throwing out.

From that experience, I realized that I had to stay true to myself and that moving forward I would create projects that reflected my direction – not what everyone else thought I *should* be doing. I've put out four other

As important as it is not to let other people's expectations of you define who you are, it's also really important not to put expectations on other people.

albums since then, and always the same thing – some people have loved them and some people have hated them. That will never change. The same now goes for my acting. And I'm sure you've experienced it in your different realms. But I'll tell you this, since I decided to let everyone else's opinions stay their own and not become mine, the *process* of creating records and of getting into character or into any other project I take on has gotten a lot more enjoyable and authentic.

Sticking to your vision is as much about the lessons along the journey as it is about what happens at the destination. In striving for greatness, we learn problem-solving skills; we learn how to be resourceful and how to anticipate and hurdle obstacles. Moving towards our vision forces us to reach down and pull out reserves of confidence we didn't know we had. We learn resilience and healing, strategy and patience. Greatness is more than the end result; the journey to get there makes you great as well.

<<REWIND

You've heard "misery loves company"? That's why, many times, people attack people who want to defy stereotypes and expectations and move forward on their own. If you start succeeding and people are hating on you, that's on them, not you.

Exercise 4: **Dig Into That bucket**

1. Have you ever felt like a crab in a bucket in your life? If so, break it down – what happened? Were you the one climbing out, or one of the other crabs in the bucket? How did this experience make you feel?

_____

_____

_____

_____

_____

_____

2. What are some techniques you can use when people try to stop you from succeeding?

_____

_____

_____

_____

_____

_____

5: UNDERDOG MENTALITY

"No one can make you feel inferior without your consent."

— ELEANOR ROOSEVELT

For me, as an artist, being Canadian automatically made me an underdog. Being neighbours to the United States, which has three hundred million people compared to Canada's thirty million, it's hard not to feel like an underdog, especially if you're a professional athlete or an artist or otherwise involved in entertainment fields.

The border between our countries is an imaginary line, yet Canadians often let it stop us like an invisible force field. There's a lot more American media than Canadian (and at least until recently it tended to be more entertaining). So a lot of our influences and ideals come from south of the forty-ninth parallel.

I was once on a panel at a high school in Scarborough to discuss the topic of how media affects youth. I thought they were looking at the wrong subject, 'cause to me it should've been specifically how American media affects Canadian youth. I say that because hanging above this panel was a banner of about six musicians, and all of them were American except one (Avril Lavigne). Generally speaking, it is believed that you haven't really "made it" until you've succeeded in the States. Part of that comes down to simple numbers. Even though Canada has the second-largest land mass in the world (after Russia), population-wise, it's a tiny country. That means the market is small, when you compare it on a North American or even on a global scale. Unfortunately, in many cases our sense of inferiority goes further than population numbers; somehow we individually and collectively buy into the expectation that Canada is "less than" in other ways.

This is what I call the "underdog mentality" – the assumption that just because you're smaller or newer or less-established or different, you're not as good as the "top dog." What's funny is that you have to be different, you need to be unique to have an edge on your competition, like we talked about when you were defining your goals. So really, by having an underdog mentality – by thinking you are less than the top dog – you're indirectly putting yourself in an inferior position.

Now let's be clear about this – there's a difference between being an underdog and having an underdog mentality. The two don't necessarily go hand in hand. An underdog is the person, team, or organization that is deemed likely to lose, usually based on a previous track record or the lack of one. At the core of it, it's not a negative thing – it's just based on statistics or odds, which as you know are not 100 per cent. The underdog mentality, on the other hand, is negative. Like I said earlier, it's the belief that you're less than or not good enough.

The story of David and Goliath is a great example of what I'm talking about here. The Israelites and Philistines were at war. Goliath, a Philistine soldier who was nine feet tall, was feared by the Israelites – he was regarded by all as the "top dog." David, an Israelite, was a young shepherd and the furthest thing from a soldier. Well, one day David heard Goliath running his mouth and he decided he would step to the giant. David ignored the advice and warnings from everyone; he had faith that he could do it (in his case, his faith was in God, but call it what you want – "source," "higher power," "inner self"). Goliath had a huge sword and was decked out in heavy armour – armour that probably weighed more than David. But little David chose not to wear armour or wield a sword, as he had never used the gear before and was unsure of his abilities. His weapon of choice was the slingshot. So David aimed the slingshot and pulled back the pocket (that stretchy rubber thing that launches the rock). The stone went flying and hit Goliath, smack, right between his eyes. The giant went down and David ran over, grabbed Goliath's sword, and sliced his head off. End of story.

The underdog mentality can be convenient, because it's an easy excuse if you fail. "The odds were against me all along." Well, who decided on those odds anyway? If that's what you're thinking, remember that you're the one who chose to believe the hype about the top dog in the first place.

To overcome your challenges, you need to tap into your own creativity and embrace yourself, especially your uniqueness, and the community around you. I'm from Toronto and I'm a fan of local artists. I buy a lot of Canadian music, first of all because a lot of it's dope, and second, because it makes me feel good to support someone from my country and especially from my city. Canadian musicians may not sell as many albums as their American counterparts, who get the benefit of multi-million dollar marketing and promotion budgets, but they're just as good or even better than anyone else and I feel proud of the fact that they come from my backyard.

No matter who we are or where we come from, we often measure our success by whether somebody bigger or more successful acknowledges us or approves of us.

There were several times I said to myself growing up, "Why couldn't I have been born in New York?" or "Why did my folks move to Toronto from Guyana, instead of to Brooklyn, like my aunts and uncles did?" It's not just a Canada/U.S. thing; it could be a neighbourhood or city thing too.

Back in the late 70s and early 80s, when hip hop was in its infancy, you had to be from New York to be considered credible. And in the country music industry, the place to be is Nashville.

Speaking of Nashville, recently I was fortunate enough to meet and kick it with country music superstar Johnny Reid. We met at the Calgary Stampede in 2009 and connected instantly (it didn't hurt that he admitted he was a Maestro fan back in the day). He was born in Scotland and raised in Toronto – neither place known as a breeding ground for country music. He was definitely an underdog but he didn't have that debilitating mentality. He packed up his family and headed south to Nashville, despite the fact that everyone told him there were already a million good country singers in Nashville. Anyway, as I write this, Johnny has just collected five Canadian Country Music Awards – so I think you can figure out how his story went.

To overcome your challenges, you need to tap into your own creativity and embrace yourself, especially your uniqueness, and the community around you.

I know it's frustrating when you feel that the skills you're blessed with can't get developed to the fullest in your backyard; this can definitely put you in the underdog position, maybe even to the point where there's no game in your neighbourhood. I have to admit I felt that many times growing up. But you see, the thing is, I never adopted the underdog mentality. I never thought I was less-than. I knew that even though I wasn't from New York City, I was just as good as any MC from the Big Apple. So don't count yourself out;

don't give up on your vision. Do your research and create or find the right playing field.

<<REWIND

In a lot of cases, people are labelled underdogs based on their history or accomplishments so far, their own lack of experience or profile, or others' prejudices. Underdogs are placed in a box because of other people's ideas (and insecurities), not because of their own ability or inability. Most times being an underdog is really about being less established or recognized and not about being less skilled or talented.

Exercise 5: How Has the Underdog Mentality Affected You?

1. What internalized assumptions do you have that have led you to believe you're "less than" another person or group of people?

_____

_____

_____

_____

_____

_____

2. Whose expectations led you to start believing that?

_____

_____

_____

_____

_____

_____

3. How does your underdog mentality affect the way you look at your vision and future?

_____

_____

_____

_____

_____

_____

4. Now turn the underdog mentality around and brainstorm all the things that you can do in your position that someone bigger or better known couldn't. How are you going to turn these things into signature features for you?

_____

_____

_____

_____

_____

_____

_____

6: DEFINING YOUR VISION

*"The reason most people never reach their
goals is that they don't define them, or ever
seriously consider them as believable or
achievable. Winners can tell you where they
are going, what they plan to do along the
way, and who will be sharing the adventure
with them."*

— DENIS WAITLEY

t's important to really understand how, up until now,
you've been bombarded with messages about what
you *can* and *can't* do and who you *should* or *shouldn't*
be. These messages have subconsciously shaped the way
you think about yourself and the expectations you place
on yourself and for your life. All these outside ideas can
interfere with your focus and make it difficult or seem-
ingly impossible to see your vision clearly. I hope that
you really take to heart the lessons I learned that I have
shared with you in the previous chapters.

So now that you're aware of how you may be limited by society or subconsciously by yourself, it's time to "blow away blockades and barricades" (I had to throw that in for all my "Backbone" fans) and create your true vision.

Vision

Your vision is the experience you want to have when you reach your destination. It's not the same as a dream because most times a dream comes to you passively, without you taking action. A vision is a motivating, forward-moving intention. A vision gets you going, while a dream keeps you imagining what could be until it finally turns into what could have been.

A vision is not quite the same as a goal, either. A goal is – like in sports – a single achievement, a moment in time. Don't get me wrong, it's important to have goals on the way to your vision. But a goal is just a factor of the equation that is your vision.

Your vision isn't your map. It's a GPS. It shows you what direction to go in, and if you go off course, it helps you calculate another route to get to where you want to be. I'm not going to tell you how to get

Destination is an experience, not a place.

you how to get from where you are to where you want to be, because I don't know your circumstances. What I do know is that whatever plan you put in place, somewhere along the line, things are going to change. If you don't know your destination, how are you going to know which detours to take?

Your vision is about how you want to live your life
– including your choice in career, whether you want
to remain single or have a family, how you want to
spend your free time, where
you want to live, and the values
and beliefs that guide you
along the way.

> Goals are milestones on the way to achieving your vision.

Do you want to be a high-powered executive who
lives in a penthouse and drives a sports car, vacations
three times a year, and dates casually? Do you want to be
a farmer who lives off the land and has a big family and
attends church daily? As you evolve as a person, so too
will your vision.

When I was nineteen years old, my vision was to
have the first big hip hop tune out of Toronto. I wanted
to be that cat who local DJs would spin in the mix while
they were playing the hottest record from New York.

When that actually happened, it was a major accomplishment for me. But I didn't stop there. I went on to
achieve many other personal and professional successes
as an MC and it was because of them that I decided to
challenge myself to grow in another arena – acting.

To tell you the truth, when I first started acting I
didn't have much of a vision besides expanding my
presence in the entertainment industry. But as I took
classes and started sharpening my skills, my vision as a
thespian became clearer.

I remember sitting with my talent agent at a restaurant in downtown Toronto after shooting the first
season of my TV series *The Line*, discussing whether

my performance on the show was worthy of a Gemini Award nomination.

That was when I realized my vision had changed from wanting to have the biggest hip hop song in my city to aspiring to be one of the most talented and respected actors in my country.

In the process of all this, I got married and had a son. So my vision expanded and now includes being the best father and husband I can possibly be. I constantly strive towards making a good life for my family and they are involved in the decisions I make. I know that what I do now affects my family as well. My role as a patriarch also influences my ideals about my music and acting career; it's not just about achieving personal goals any more. It's about providing a certain quality of life for me and my family. Yeah, I'd jump at a seven-figure movie role, but if it was going to take me away from my family for six months, I'd really have to evaluate how it plays into my overall vision, not just how it fits with my professional goals.

Professions will change. Interests will develop and expand. But as long as you're sticking to the belief that you are destined for greatness, no matter what obstacles get in your way, you will be ready to face those challenges and to *Stick to Your Vision*.

Stay Flexible

Knowing the experience you want to have allows you to stay flexible yet focused on your destination. You know you want to be in the end zone, but if you think there's only one way to get there, you're never going to make it.

You need to determine what things you can compromise on and what things you can't. Your values will guide you as your journey takes its twists and turns; we will work on defining them at the end of this chapter.

It takes a lot of heart to challenge the odds and pursue your passion. It can be intimidating to take career risks and face uncertainty, and not everyone is willing to take that "leap of faith." Respect is due to you for giving it a shot, because you're already a hundred times ahead of the pack who wants to stay in the safe zone.

The Vision of a Rappin' Mortician

Not long ago, I drove from Vancouver up to a show in Whistler, B.C., and shared my ride with one of the opening acts, a cool brother by the name of Godfrey Young. I knew he had a day job, because we couldn't leave till he'd finished work.

So on the way up, I asked him what his main hustle was. Dude told me he was a mortician. I said, a *what?* He repeated himself. I was like, okay, that's cool. I never met a rappin' mortician before. I asked him what exactly his job entailed. My man said everything from consulting and comforting the families to embalming or cremating the body, sometimes writing the obituary, the eulogies . . . everything that had to do with death.

What are you doing or saying that no one else is?

It really kind of bugged me out, 'cause here I was, on this ninety-minute drive, listening to some old-school hip hop, and just trying to start a conversation. Then my man

BTW: Don't Aim for Fame

If "being famous" is your vision, go back and do the exercises again. Fame is a by-product — it's the result of achieving a goal and doing it well — it's not the actual objective. It's not that you can't have celebrity as part of your vision; it's that if you're looking to be a celebrity without any other goals, you're probably driven more by your ego than by your passion. You need to examine your motivation for wanting fame. Is it because the media makes it look so cool? Maybe you think it'll solve all your problems. That's not a positive reason: you're running away from something instead of aspiring to something.

And don't get it twisted. Fame comes at a high price. It can put you out there for divine scrutiny and make people think they have the right to judge you. It can also mean you lose your anonymity, and although it's flattering to be recognized and get props in public, it's also nice to be able to walk through the mall without being jumped on by an amped fan.

As my homie Big Sleeps says, "Props (that come with fame) don't pay the bills — they cost you."

Godfrey hit me in the head with his occupation. What he was telling me was so interesting, I had to turn down the Special Ed tune I was listening to so I could hear more. He told me that in order to get his job he had to get educated in a lot of different areas, like he had to learn about a variety of religions and cultures, because each one has different traditions, beliefs, and ceremonies around death. On top of that, he had to have a great way with people, because he was dealing with grieving family members and friends at one of the worst times of their lives.

He told me the story of a funeral he organized for a motorcyclist who was killed in a bike accident. He coordinated it so hundreds of riders would ride in on their bikes, and as the hearse was pulling away to go back to the funeral home, the riders would all simultaneously rev their engines and burn their tires in honour of the fallen motorcyclist. The stunt team then joined the funeral procession, pulling catwalks and performing stunts all the way back to the funeral home. Godfrey said it was the type of service that sent chills up and down your spine and that the cat's friends and family were very pleased with his support and creativity in this time of tragedy.

I asked him how he became interested in being a mortician and he told me that his mother had died in a brutal head-on collision. He explained how he'd broken down and had a very difficult time coping with it, and that the turning point had been when he met the guy who was there preparing the funeral. The mortician was so accommodating and supportive, Godfrey said. He'd really needed the consolation and comfort the mortician had offered – his support had truly been a gift.

At that point, Godfrey realized what his calling was: to help people through a life-altering crisis.

So he went to school, taking courses for all the skills he would need in his new occupation. He's now so well respected that he's in high demand. He makes a huge difference in people's lives.

You never know what's going to happen to help you find your calling. It is important to act once you figure it out. Godfrey Young is a great example of someone who found his calling, listened to what his career was telling him to do, set his goals, and acted on them. On the weekend my man thrashes other MCs, and during the week he's a mortician who provides comfort and support to grieving families. It may seem like an odd combo but it works for him.

The Bad and Good News

The bad news: Unless you time-travel back to the 1970s and are a son of Guyanese immigrants who wants to be a rapper in a country that doesn't have any, I can't tell you *exactly* how to achieve your vision.

The good news: What I can tell you are some of the challenges I faced, and I think most people face, how I dealt with them, and some ways you can think about dealing with them.

Without a clear vision, you can read this book as many times as you want, but you're going nowhere. Fast. Writing down your vision is key. Even writing this book made me realize again how important it is to put your thoughts down on paper. By conceptualizing the three sections of Expectation, Operation, and Destination, I created the right tone and the foundation for the book. Once things were written on paper, it made it easier for me to explain my vision to the publishers, McClelland & Stewart. I knew what I wanted and knew how to explain it to others because the skeletal plan was already mapped out. At the end of the chapter you'll find an exercise to get you started.

Dedication driven by passion can lead to greatness.

<<REWIND

Understanding that your expectations of yourself have been influenced by ideas and limitations placed on you by others is essential in breaking free and determining your real vision. Your vision is a guide that helps direct your life towards your destination.

Exercise 6: Clarifying Your Vision

1. *Look for your inspiration.*

It helps to go somewhere that inspires you, wherever that is. It could be a bench in the park, a quiet corner in a library, or just somewhere with a great view, like the place I used to go. I would drive to the Scarborough Bluffs, the cliffs along part of the shoreline of Lake Ontario. I'd sit by the rocks, feel the cool breeze on my face, and I would catch a vibe. It was nothing fancy – I'd use a pen and paper and just start writing lyrics for a new song or rehearsing lines for an upcoming role or audition. The point was just to plan out my next moves. Once I got going, I found that ideas would start flowing. It's important to find time for just *you*.

Some folks are morning people, and they get pumped by the sun rising over the hills or the city or the ocean. Some are night owls, and their creativity starts flowing after midnight. The bottom line is you need to find a time and a place to block everything out for a little while, just enough time to make some notes or draw your own personal map, and then you're good. Avoid all the thoughts of "I should" or "My parents want me to" or "People will laugh at me." This time is for *your* thoughts, not anyone else's.

2. *Create your personal mission statement.*

While you're setting your goals, it's important to know who you are. This will help you be more on point and realistic.

Write down three things that define you as an individual. Doing this is really important because it will help you set expectations for yourself. You don't have to write them in any specific order but put down three things that are part of your essence: they should be adjectives that you would list as attributes on your resumé, such as punctual, hard-working, innovative, etc.

It was important for me to write down these three things. It took time to figure them out, but once I did, it helped me a lot. It's a good reference point for me when I'm setting out goals for specific projects.

Take some time, and when you're done, carry on reading and I'll tell you what I wrote down.

a) _____

b) _____

c) _____

The three essential things about me are longevity, perseverance, and my heritage.

Here's why those are my three things, and how they've shown up in my vision.

a) Longevity. My community has given me a lot of love and support throughout the last twenty years. I've been representing T-Dot since before the CN Tower was built, and people still thank me for what I do. Yeah, I'm older and wiser now, but I never quit. So longevity is an appropriate attribute for me.

b) Perseverance. Over my career, I have had to reinvent myself a few times. I went from being hugely popular in hip hop to almost irrelevant, and it's real easy to just give up and say, "I used to be . . ." That doesn't work for me. I've expanded my skills and made some positive career transitions since I came up. Film and television have been good to me, and my acting skills are improving. That makes me proud, and it keeps me motivated. I'm not Denzel Washington yet but I'm doing my thing.

c) My heritage. Growing up as an ethnic minority in a country that's overshadowed by the United States, I felt it was (and still feel it is) really important to know my heritage – my Guyanese heritage, my black heritage, my Canadian heritage, my musical heritage. Being an ethnic minority and learning about the various aspects of my heritage has been a lifelong process.

3. *Elaborate on your personal mission statement.*
Go ahead and write out the reasons you chose the three things that define you. Just a few sentences, so you're clear on what you mean by a particular word or phrase.

a) _____

_____

b) _____

_____

c) _____

_____

I keep my personal mission statement in mind when I'm making important decisions. For example, when I'm doing business with companies, I try to work with those that have longevity, have persevered through adversity, or are connected to their heritage.

In the past I've organized events that have been sponsored by Molson Canadian, Canada's oldest brewery. Molson epitomizes all three of my defining qualities – longevity (oldest Canadian brewery), perseverance (obviously, to make it this far), and heritage (just look at their name – Molson *Canadian*).

4. *Identify your passion.*
What do you really love to do? What gets you amped up every time you think about it? That's where you're going to find your vision. It takes a hell of a lot of hard work to persevere through the tough times and setbacks, and the way you're going to survive is by having absolute passion for what you do.

So write down three activities you'd do even if they didn't make you a penny:

a) _____

b) _____

c) _____

Some people say you should pick what you're great at, what you do better than anybody else. If that thing happens to be your passion too, you're laughing. But most of the time, dedication driven by passion can lead to greatness. You don't necessarily have to be great off the bat.

When I started out as an MC, I always rhymed too fast. I was ahead of the beat all the time. And to be a great MC you need to have a "tight flow," so I had to practise my rhymes a lot, especially slowing them down.

5. Find your uniqueness

It's essential for you to know what makes you stand out from everyone else. *What is it that you are doing or saying that no one else is?* It doesn't matter what field you're in, you can either compete or create. Competing means you're doing the same thing as everybody else and hustling to try and do it better. Creating means you're carving out a place for yourself.

It can take a lot of time to figure out what you can do that's different, but if you take the time now, it'll make some things a whole lot easier down the road.

_____

_____

_____

_____

_____

_____

6. *Visualize your destination experience.*

First off, fast-forward to the time when you truly feel you've reached your destination and visualize what you want your life to look like. And when I say visualize, I mean you really have to experience it – use all your senses. What does it taste like? What does it smell like? How does it make you feel?

Take two (or more) pages in your Vision Book and write out what your perfect day would be like, from the time you wake up until the time you go to bed.

Who is with you? Where do you live? What kind of work are you doing? Who do you work with? What opportunities and challenges have you had? What's the biggest challenge you're facing? Remember to think about everything and everyone that's important to you or your vision.

If you're like me and write music, you may prefer to write a song that describes your perfect day. Or grab a magazine and collage something that reflects it. Paint it! Write a play or short story. Express it your way. There are no rules on how to do this except do it your way and be vivid in your detail.

Now you've got it – that's your vision, or at least the beginnings of it.

TWO: **OPERATION**

"I didn't roll out of bed and direct *Malcolm* X. Whatever you do, go out there and work hard."

— SPIKE LEE

Overleaf: Performing "Let Your Backbone Slide" at a private party in Montreal. (Photo by Lorne Shereck, 2009)

TALKIN' WINDOWS: PART TWO

S o you decide to check out the third window. The conversation continues and it goes like this:

YOU:
Okay, I decided to stick around. Tell me something good.

WINDOW NUMBER THREE:
All I'm saying is after you set your vision, you have to trick your brain and get your mind right. You need to know in your heart that complacency and mediocrity are beneath you. Then you need to plan out your actions. You're going to need some tools. And also, think about the people you know, or need to meet, who can help you.

YOU:
What do you mean?

WINDOW NUMBER THREE:
I mean, how resourceful can you be to get through this? This takes discipline and focus. You need to develop your skills to make sure you can use all the tools in your toolbelt. You gotta surround yourself with the right people. If the people you hang with are messin' with those two other windows, you have to let them go or at least give them a break for a while.

YOU:
For real?

WINDOW NUMBER THREE:
Yeah, for real. If people you kick it with aren't trying to get through this too, and they're not striving for excellence, they are a liability to you. You don't have time to waste, my man. Surround yourself with the folks who can actually help you use your tools. Folks who will try to get through this window – and if they can't, they will try to break down the damn door!

To be continued...

7: **GET MOVING**

"Vision without action is a dream. Action without vision is simply passing the time. Action with vision is making a positive difference."
— JOEL A. BARKER

Now you've got a vision and you understand some of the road blocks you might face. So how do you get from here to your destination?

After your vision is all written out, you've got to get out there and make it happen. Don't *tell* me what you're going to do. Just get out there and do the damn thing. I have a couple friends who, if they did only half of the things they talk about doing, would be rollin' with Bill Gates. After a while, I stopped taking them seriously, because no matter how great their ideas were, I knew they weren't going to do anything with them.

I don't like to talk too much about what I'm *going to do*. I like to *just do it* (big up to Nike). It's much more rewarding that way. If you spend time talking about it, people might put expectations on you, and if those are negative expectations ("Nah, you'll never be able to do that, man"), you may run the risk of starting to believe the haters and lowering your expectations of yourself. Then you won't do what you were planning, and your critics will say, "See? I told you you'd never do it." Then you might start to constantly second-guess yourself. If you begin putting your ideas into action, you'll feel good about yourself. I'm telling you, there's no feeling like starting a project, getting on a roll, and feeling a sense of accomplishment. Nobody will be able to say "You can't do that" – because you're already doing it!

Action creates motivation.

Success isn't only about what you do; it's also about having the right mindset. In addition to *doing* things, there are certain *ways of thinking* you need to succeed, and if they're not already part of your personality, you're going to have to work on developing them. For people who have deeply ingrained habits of negative thinking, self-criticism, or playing it safe, it may take a lot of work. But developing a winning mindset will serve you well in the different facets of your life: at work, in your home and your relationships, and so on.

Putting It in Motion

Once people see you initiating your plan and making progress, they're going to start respecting you. Even if they don't think you can accomplish it, they know you deserve props. Who knows, they may even offer you some advice or help steer you in the right direction. And

I met Drake five years ago or so. I was filming *Instant Star* and he was filming *Degrassi: The Next Generation*. The same company produced both shows, so the cast members intermingled from time to time. One day, when I was wrapping up filming, he walked into our shared dressing room, big grin on his face.

He told me his music was coming together, that he was working with some cats from the States. He's a laid-back dude, but he was amped; I remember how excited he looked, telling me this.

I was surprised, because I only knew him as an actor; I had no idea he was an MC/singer.

I knew he had skills when I heard a few of his early songs on mix tapes, but to see his career pop off like this internationally makes a brother smile.

He's got songs on *Billboard*, he's collaborated with everyone from Mary J. Blige to Jay-Z and Lil Wayne, and he just got nominated for two Grammys . . . all this before putting out his first album. That's groundbreaking.

Although Drake is much younger than I am, he has inspired me because he is the ultimate example of what can happen when you Stick to Your Vision. He knew he wanted to be a recording artist, and although Canada is not exactly the home of platinum-selling hip hop record labels, he didn't let that stop him. He continued hustling, putting more mix tapes on the Internet as well as doing some serious collaborations, and the rest is history.

remember that nothing's going to happen overnight. Most of us had to crawl, walk, then run – in that order. That's the process of growth. I've come a long way from dropping off demo tapes at reception desks. I learned through experience how to set more precise goals so my plan of action can be more on point. But I'm still going to make more mistakes, and I'll continue to grow and learn from them.

Know that it's part of the growth process, learn from your mistakes . . . and then be better. No matter what, *just keep doing your thing*.

Motivation

Most people think motivation is something that strikes you like lightning. They sit around saying "I'm not motivated" and use that as an excuse for not getting anything done. Guess what? They keep sitting there and sitting there, and nothing gets done. Their vision becomes a memory.

I'll let you in on a little something: Action creates motivation. Get started – do something, anything, related to your goal, and you'll be surprised. Doing something makes you feel good, proud. Feeling good makes you want to do more. So you do more and feel even better. You're motivated because you know how good it's going to feel when you accomplish the next step.

There have been so many times I've wanted to write a song but I just couldn't figure out where to begin. I'd get writer's block. Damn, I hate when that happens. It's like, you're ready to start vibing, but no words come to mind, and you can't recite or write anything.

I composed a dope beat (for a track that I later ended up calling "I'm Drinking Milk Now") but I couldn't even come up with a concept for the song, let alone lyrics to go with it. I needed inspiration to get my creative juices flowing so I decided to listen to some classic rock; I wanted to hear something that was totally outside of the hip hop realm. I was really feeling the metaphors in Simon and Garfunkel's "Bridge Over Troubled Water." That song was based on the idea of someone being there for you and helping you get over troubled times, like a bridge helps you cross troubled waters. That got me thinking, and although the two aren't related, I came up with a concept about my progress and how I'd grown. I called it "I'm Drinking Milk Now" because milk helps you grow big and strong. You might not see the correlation, and there might not actually even be one, but the point is that I got out of my rut.

I can't lie, even during the process of writing this book, I encountered a little writer's block here and there. There were times when I got stuck on how to word something, or even what to write next, and I'd get frustrated. I'd fight to spit out the words and they just wouldn't come. So one day I decided that instead of struggling and losing precious writing time, I would instead work on a "Shoutout." This was perfect because it allowed me to switch gears but still contribute to the overall completion of the project. So I would do this every time I got stuck. And usually once I finished writing a "Shoutout" about somebody, I was able to pick up right where I had left off, which was encouraging.

You know what I'm talking about – it's like that feeling you have when you finally get around to cleaning your place. It's not the most fun activity, but it sure feels good when you see the progress – and the floor of your bedroom. So good, in fact, that you don't just stop at your bedroom, but you hit the kitchen, the living room, and the bathroom. How can something so small give you such a rush? It's that sense of accomplishment that keeps you moving forward . . . even if you don't like cleaning.

Here's another secret: Keep your step-by-step goals small. It's easy to become overwhelmed when you have a huge vision like "become CEO of a Fortune 500 company" or "become the next Lil Wayne or Jay-Z." Start with something simple, like researching courses on corporate leadership or calling the local club to see if they have an open mic show (that's how I started out back in the day).

The rule of thumb is that each sub-task you set for yourself should take three to five minutes. I know you're thinking, "Wes, I can't get anything done in five minutes! I might as well give up . . . and sit here on the couch *talking* about my great ideas."

Wrong.

Try this: think of something you need to do that you haven't done because you didn't feel like it. Change the oil in your car, get your laundry together, clean the bathroom, gather all the garbage and put it outside, weed the garden . . . whatever it is you've been putting off. If you have the cleanest place with a perfect garden, no garbage, and fresh oil in the car, alphabetize your CD collection (remember those things?).

Feel better? More motivated?

That's how it works. Start something, anything, productive.

Just get off your ass and do something.

<<REWIND

Don't let your vision become a memory. Create your own motivation by taking small steps towards your vision. This will get you moving in the right direction and create momentum. Motivation can come from the most unlikely places or activities – even something as boring as cleaning your room.

Exercise 7: **Baby Steps**

Now that you have described your destination in your
Vision Book, it's time to take the first baby step toward
it. You decide what it is. Even if it's just doing some
research, and not an actual physical step, do it. Google,
call a professional or an association, research a course,
sign up on Facebook, MySpace, or some other social
networking site to promote your talent or product. Just
start at the beginning. And write this down in your
Vision Book.

8: SELF-ESTEEM AND CONFIDENCE

*"If you have no confidence in self, you
are twice defeated in the race of life.
With confidence, you have won even
before you have started."*
                    — MARCUS GARVEY

I cannot stress enough the importance of cultivating confidence and high self-esteem. I believe that self-esteem is the general opinion you have about your worthiness – you either hold yourself in high regard or low regard. Low self-esteem plagues you with an over-all feeling of insignificance. High self-esteem leads you to feel competent and deserving. This is a quality that will help you strive to be the best, the greatest, you can possibly be. You need to have a positive sense of worth in order to set high expectations for yourself. When your self-esteem is high, it gives you that energy to strive towards excellence, to handle setbacks, and to get up and keep going.

In this media age we're bombarded with so many different messages about what it takes to be cool or accepted; it can be difficult to feel good about yourself if you don't match what society says you're supposed to be. It goes back to what I said about growing up and only seeing negative reflections of yourself on TV or from the people around you – you are less likely to feel good about yourself.

Some people grow up hearing negative things about themselves so often they start to believe them. Think back to what I said about your expectations of yourself

BTW: "Backbone" Storyboard

I already knew exactly what I wanted the video for "Let Your Backbone Slide" to look like long before we even shot it. So when I met with the video director, Joel Goldberg, it was easy for me to explain to him what I wanted. We met at a restaurant to discuss the treatment for the video, and I drew it on a napkin. Little did I know that Joel would save that napkin for over twenty years. So when I reached out to him to talk about writing this book, he e-mailed me a scan of that napkin. Even two decades later I feel such a sense of pride when I see my scribbles and how they came alive in that video. Peep the storyboard here and check out the video on YouTube or whatever. And P.S. – the ideas we didn't use from the storyboard for the "Backbone" video were later used in the video for "Drop the Needle," which ended up winning a Juno for Best Video.

—Light comes on the Maestro as he completes writing the Masterpiece. "This jam is amplified... Let Your Backbone Slide."

—Fellas dancing at a party. "On the left... (The Chorus)."

"You listen to every word I say... Hiphop Tic-Taction" (walking through crowd)

A close-up of the 'Masterpiece' in The Maestro's hand. "A Rap is like a slab of clay... "

"Universe without light..." Maestro at the desk with 2 girls dancing behind him.

"Sun could be shining" Dancers

– lots of people internalize what others expect or say. They assume that because they heard X so much, X must be true. These people can become adolescents and adults who constantly get down on themselves for every little thing and this can be so paralyzing it prevents them from reaching their destination.

You can do many things to boost your self-esteem; but it's a personal thing. What raises one person's self-esteem might not make a difference to another person. You need to figure out what works for you.

Expressing Yourself

It's important for people, especially young people, to find something they are passionate about and to develop that interest. Learning to and being able to express yourself artistically, athletically, or in business can help you develop confidence, build upon your strengths and weaknesses, and develop your self-esteem.

It's empowering to create something, to watch it grow from a single concept in your mind and take shape in the world. It doesn't have to be recognized internationally; you don't have to win the Nobel Prize for it. Just the fact that you thought of an idea, you thought about how to make it happen, and then took the steps to make it a reality, that is going to give you a huge sense of accomplishment. A painter who recreates on canvas the wild colours he sees in his mind; the inventor who sees something that doesn't yet exist and has an idea how to create it; the chef who slices and dices and creates a culinary masterpiece – those are beautiful things.

The more you create, the more opportunities you'll have to surprise yourself with just how amazing you can be. Once the creative energies are flowing you'll find your "zone," where ideas and answers seem to come to you from out of the blue. And don't be shy about taking a moment to appreciate the results of your efforts. When I wrote the song "Built to Last," I was on a roll – the lyrics just flowed onto my notepad. After I finished, I recited it to myself. I mean this with all humility, but I got misty-eyed when I realized how much *I* appreciated it. I surprised myself, writing something so lyrically dope. I had a moment.

Learning to and being able to express yourself artistically, athletically, or in business can help you develop confidence, build upon your strengths and weaknesses, and develop your self-esteem.

One of the biggest self-esteem enhancers is being able to sit back and feel proud of what you created – especially if it comes out better than you actually expected.

Like all young people, though, I had to find what gave me *confidence*, which is a different thing. I define confidence as the belief in yourself or your capabilities.

I had good self-esteem in high school, but I had to find what made me feel confident or sure of myself. I played football, and that helped me learn many things that are essential to success – teamwork, getting back up after a loss, discipline, responsibility – all the important things. I knew I wasn't headed for the NFL, but because I love football, it wasn't about that.

All those lessons I learned from sports I was able to use in my career in music. And that's where it was at for me.

As a youngster I dabbled in breakdancing, because that was the thing in the 1980s, but every time I tried to break, I looked like a clown. I'd attempt hand spins and land on my face. Moves like that are not sexy. What's worse, the breakers got all the girls, so I was embarrassed *and* jealous. Determined to get the girls, I focused even harder on my rhymes.

When I was starting out rhyming, I used to practise with my good friend and first DJ, Greg Nathaniel (DJ Greg). Like I mentioned earlier, I had a bad habit of rhyming faster than the track, and it frustrated Greg when I rapped out of sync with his 45s. Over and over, he'd tell me how to stay "in the pocket" with the beat. It took a lot of steady practice, but by the age of fifteen, I was getting

When your self-esteem is high, it gives you that energy to strive towards excellence, to handle setbacks, and to get up and keep going.

really nice with the verbals, and because of that, I gained a lot of confidence. I started coming up with some slick wordplay – and that's when the girls started feelin' me.

I also read a lot of magazines about hip hop culture. Both Kurtis Blow and Melle Mel said that if you weren't nice on the mic, fans would diss you hard and boo you or might even throw bottles. I definitely didn't want that to happen, so that gave me incentive to practise! I decided it would never happen to me, because I was going to be just as good as or better than they were. Whenever I was nervous, I would think about what the MCs in New York would go through. If they could do it, I could rep for Toronto and kill it. I'd say to myself, *Nobody's going to boo me because I'm too dope.*

It's natural to feel nervous, there's nothing wrong with that. But if you let that feeling overtake you, it can trap you in a box. You're buying into the possibility that you're going to fail, and if you don't take charge of those feelings they are going to knock you off point. You've got to break out of it – and it's hard, I know. Believe me, it's not that I don't get nervous; it's that I have a strategy for how to make it go away.

Check this out: Think about a person you respect and admire. Now, imagine that person's mindset. How would they act in your situation? Borrow their confidence (they

BTW: Think Positively

I have a friend who really inspires me with his courage and optimism. In 2003 he was diagnosed with bone cancer and fought it, only to have it come back in 2009. I spoke to him just after he found out it had returned.

He told me, "Wes, I'm going to beat this. This is my second time going through radiation, and I realize that the main thing with this is my mind. My mind has to be sharp. A lot of people fail; they get sick once, and they get used to being sick, or they give up. But I'm not going to let this get to me. My mind is the factor here."

I like the way he worded that. He has his vision – beating cancer – and he has to get his brain on point. He knows it's going to be tough, and he's going to feel like hell. But he's not going to let being sick immobilize or define him. He's going to think about his two beautiful daughters, and he's going to fight it.

won't mind). Be yourself, but imagine LeBron James called you up and said, "Look, I know you've got game, son, and believe me, I know what it's like to be nervous, too, so I'm going to give you some of my confidence. You can have it. This is the same   confidence I channelled in last night's game to land that three-pointer at the buzzer, all right?" If LeBron can handle the pressure on him, you can deal with a presentation to your boss. Look at it this way: at least when you make a mistake at work, fifty thousand people don't boo you. Take your mindset up a level. We're all going to get nervous, but if we're going to succeed, we have to work through it.

One of the most famous examples of the importance of practice as a way to gain confidence comes from Wayne Gretzky. From the time he was a little kid, he practised for hours a day, before and after school, all weekend, into the evenings. He knew what he wanted, and he decided he was going to make it happen – and he did.

Obviously, practice is important if you want to achieve your vision. You have to be great at what you do. But the other thing is that the more you practise, the more confidence you'll have. You'll know that you know what you're doing. So when those nerves kick in, you can talk back to them and say, "Step off, I'm the best, and I'm going to be great."

When I started rapping, I didn't have any superstar dreams. I just found something I was good at, something I loved (and something the girls loved me for).

In hip hop, I found something I believed in, and something that *validated* me – made me see that I mattered. Hip hop also kept me out of trouble, because I was putting all my energy into practising writing and rhyming.

There's an old saying that "if you believe you can do something, you're right. If you believe you can't, you're also right."

Self-esteem is essential to so many things in life: happiness, success, relationships, resilience (the ability to bounce back when things go wrong – I'll get to that later). You should be your number-one fan because you are the one who's there 24/7, and the one you've got to rely on to accomplish your goals, so cultivating self-esteem and confidence is essential (and it will make you feel better!).

If you have low self-esteem and a lack of confidence, you're shooting yourself in the foot before you even take a step. And you're less likely to take that step to begin with. What's unfortunate is that people who don't think highly enough of themselves often feel unworthy because they've been taught to feel so. People in their past have criticized them constantly, to the point where they have a running negative commentary in their head.

The good news is that no matter where you are on the spectrum, there are ways to improve your self-esteem. The better news is that you're already doing it: by having a vision and reading this book.

So let's take it a little further. Here are six more ways you can improve your self-esteem:

1. **Participate in an extracurricular activity** – I played football and liked kicking it with the fellas. Whether you're running the plays on a neighbourhood sports team or participating in a book club, interacting with others in a group situation can make you see how much you are valued. You'll also learn your strengths and develop new relationships.

2. **Affirmations** – Write out positive statements about yourself (or get a friend or family member to do this) and post them around your house or apartment. Every day, look in the mirror and say your affirmations out loud. It might sound kind of corny, but it's been proven that by changing the way you think, you can change the way you feel.

3. **Volunteer** – I've volunteered with different organizations throughout the years – Covenant House, Kids Help Phone, and Sick Kids Hospital, to name a few – and it feels good helping others. You'll recognize that you have something to offer and that you matter to other people. It also helps reinforce your values. Plus, the more you give of yourself, the more you get back.

4. **Surround yourself with positive people** – Besides my wife and son, I have friends and former co-workers I call to get a boost of energy. Positivity can be contagious, so make sure you're around

lots of it. It's difficult to wallow in self-pity when you're around people who won't stand for it and who demand better of you. Plus, you can usually count on positive people for support and encouragement.

BTW: What the Bleep Do We Know!?

In the 2004 documentary *What The Bleep Do We Know!?* there is a sequence dealing with an experiment by Japanese scientist Dr. Emoto called "Messages From Water." Basically, he typed out positive and negative words and taped the printed words onto bottles of filtered water. He took pictures of the water before the words were taped on the bottles and then after. The results were astounding – and very telling.

Under a microscope, the water in the bottles with the positive messages like "Love" and "Thank you" looked like beautiful crystals that resembled diamonds and snowflakes.

The water molecules in the bottles with the negative messages like "You make me sick" and "I will kill you" were brown and withered – they looked sick.

A man in the documentary asked, "If thoughts can do this to water, imagine what thoughts can do to us?"

And as the woman in the film noted, the human body consists of about 90 per cent water.

The experiment was highly regarded by some, while others thought it was hogwash – but check it out for yourself. Either way, it's a very cool documentary and the concepts are definitely worth pondering! You can peep it at your local video store or maybe even online.

5. **Laugh** – Comedian Russell Peters makes me laugh. So do old-school Eddie Murphy flicks. And that joint *The Hangover* is mad funny. Watch or read comedies. It feels good to laugh and it rids you of negativity and replaces it with a natural high. It helps you relax, get out of your own head, and take the focus off yourself. It can be therapeutic.

6. **Learn something new** – Take a class or get a how-to book. I was always interested in real estate so I took a course. I didn't intend to become an agent, but I was curious about the profession and thought the skills could be transferable to other areas in my life. Learning something you didn't know before gives you a great sense of satisfaction and accomplishment. Read inspiring books (like this one!) and think about what else you might want to learn.

Trick Your Mind

I was at a prep meeting for a speaking engagement in Vancouver last year. I walked out of the building with one of the hosts, Marving Marisca, and we were discussing the premise of this book, which I was still writing at the time. He said, "Wes, what you're talking about really inspires me. The brain is so powerful, man. What I've done is, I've tricked my mind. I'm thinking in a completely different way than I used to." This guy was twenty-two years old, he's from Africa, and he used

I met Steve Nash in a place you wouldn't expect: a party in Toronto during Fashion Week 2000. I didn't recognize him at first – I thought he was in a rock band or something – and it wasn't till we began talking about the NBA that I clued in.

This cat was mad humble and very appreciative of his success. It's not every day a dude from Victoria, Canada, becomes a starting NBA point guard – much less wins League MVP two years in a row. Now, I'm a big Shaquille O'Neal fan, but I had to smile when a fellow Canadian beat him out for the MVP title.

I'm inspired by Steve's work ethic and belief in himself – and by the fact that he breaks the mould: Not all professional Canadian athletes have to be NHL stars!

to work at a gas station when he first moved to Canada. Then one day he decided he wanted more out of life. So he set his vision, moved on, and now he's got a cool government job. And he's still reaching higher, still working hard to learn more so he can move up and tackle other challenges.

Your brain is your best ally, but if it's telling you negative things, it can be your worst enemy, too. So you've got to work around your negative thoughts. I've known that and talked about it for years, but the way he said it was perfect: "I've tricked my mind." When negative energy and thoughts come in, trick your brain

Tricking your mind means deleting the negative thoughts and inserting positive thoughts.

to think positive thoughts. I know it can be hard but try not to even let negative words come out of your mouth. You know the old saying, "If you can't say anything good, don't say anything at all"? Tricking your brain would be taking that one step further – "If you can't say anything good, say something better." When we are in adversarial situations or just feeling down, bad vibes can easily take us over, so they need to be replaced with good ones. The thing is, you don't even have to believe the good thoughts, not at first anyway, you just need to play the opposite game – replace the negative thought with a completely opposite thought. Tricking your mind means deleting the negative thoughts and inserting positive thoughts. Do this every time a dark cloud rolls through your mind and it will just become habit. By the time this habit is engrained, you will believe the good thoughts. Boom, you've tricked your mind.

<<REWIND

Self-esteem and confidence are both necessary to keep you going on the road to your destination. Volunteering and working with others, including participating in extracurricular activities, are great ways to improve your sense of self. Tricking your brain from thinking negative thoughts to thinking positive thoughts helps you focus on achieving your vision.

Exercise 8: **Create Your Own Mantra**

Come up with a sentence or phrase that amps you up, boosts your confidence, and reminds you of your destination. Write it in your Vision Book, or even set it to music and hum it as your own personal theme song. And then get some sticky notes and write it on them . . . and put the notes where you'll see them – the kitchen fridge, the bathroom mirror, your bedroom dresser. And most importantly, remember to read and recite this phrase everyday, several times a day, as often as you can.

9: TAKING RISKS

"A ship in the harbor is safe but that's not
what ships are built for."

– LEE SILBER

Taking risks is essential for everybody, and it helps us grow and develop confidence in ourselves. It's scary, sure, but either you're going to succeed or you're going to learn something that will help you succeed the next time. And what if you don't succeed the first time? It may be a bitter feeling, but by regrouping and analyzing your mistakes – doing a personal play-by-play review – you become better at what you do and you become stronger. Every time we fail and then regroup, we learn the importance of having patience and of trying to understand ourselves and those around us. It is natural to try something a few times before succeeding; the key is to bounce right back and not to be fearful of making the same mistake – because you won't. Being afraid to fail is being afraid to succeed.

My son is just learning that there's a faster way to get around than crawling. He sees his mother and me walking around, and all the other big people, and every time he's sitting on the floor, he pushes himself up and tries to walk. So far, he's fallen down every single time. He doesn't feel afraid or embarrassed or self-conscious. He just gets right back up and wobbles again. And you know what? Because he keeps trying, one of these days, my little man is going to walk.

Being afraid to fail is being afraid to succeed.

Here's one of the risks I took:

While I was still struggling to get noticed as an MC, in 1988, I said to myself, "I don't care what anybody thinks, I'm going to get a record deal and I'm going to put Toronto on the hip hop map."

My grand plan was to drop off some demo tapes to receptionists at a bunch of rap labels in New York. Now, anybody who's been anywhere near the entertainment industry knows that's not going to do a damn thing for you, but I had no clue what the correct procedure was. I just knew I wasn't going to sit around waiting for somebody to give me an opportunity; I was going to make my own opportunity.

I coerced my friend and then-manager, Farley Flex (who some of you know as one of the judges on *Canadian Idol*), to drive me down. I had an aunt in Brooklyn and we would crash at her place.

It was a long drive. A really long drive – on one highway, the whole way. I'd figured once we passed

Niagara – hey, that's New York, right? – it shouldn't be hard to get there. We watched the sun set behind us, and we kept driving. The moon came up, we kept driving. Farley began singing old Stylistic tunes to stay calm.

Finally, just around the time the sun came up, we reached Brooklyn. But then we got lost. How was I supposed to know Brooklyn was so big? And that so many people lived there? One of those millions of people was my Aunt Joan and we just had to find her. She lived somewhere called Flatbush. Farley wasn't singing at this point. He wasn't in the mood to.

"A coward dies a thousand deaths, a hero but one."
– Shakespeare

"Where's the damn map?!" he said.

"Uhh, map? We've been on one damn highway for twelve hours. Didn't think we needed a *map*."

"Did you think we'd get here and you'd just magically know where your Aunt Joan's house is?"

Actually, yeah. Kind of.

Truth was, I felt like an idiot, but I was so determined to get to the New York record labels that I hadn't thought much beyond the "get to New York" part.

Even though I was naive, I was hungry, ambitious, and I believed in myself. I had set a goal for myself, and as far as I was concerned, nothing was going to stop me now that I was in the hip hop Mecca.

After turning down a few wrong streets we finally found my aunt. The next day we went to Def Jam, Island, Jive, Profile – the top rap labels – and dropped off my demo tapes. Profile Records was the only company that

BTW: Shakespeare and the Comedian

One night, I was sitting at a table in a hotel lounge in Vancouver, British Columbia, one of the places I like to go and work. The hotel is connected to a comedy club, so there are always different comics around. In comes this comedian – this guy just finished his show and wanted love; I was busy in my own world reading, but this cat was determined to start a conversation. He wouldn't stop rambling but there was one thing that he said that really stood out. "A coward dies a thousand times, but a hero only once." I thought that was kind of cool.

He said, "The reason why that quote means so much to me is because I used to kick box. I was a champion amateur martial artist."

Turns out my man was not only a competitive kick boxer, he was a kick-ass kick boxer. He went on, "I can't tell you how many people I beat kick boxing. But I will tell you this: In the tenth grade, a twelfth-grade bully hit me. I went down, and I was scared, man. I was too scared to get up and throw a single punch." He lowered his head and shook it back and forth slowly. "You know what?" He lifted his head and looked me straight in the eye. "Even if I'd swung and gotten my butt kicked, I'd be okay with it, because at least I wouldn't have been a coward." I swear, dude looked like he was going to cry. "There's so much in life, you've gotta get up and at least take a shot at the bully, whatever the bully is. Go for that, man."

That hit me hard for real. Here was this guy in his thirties, and he was still reliving what he *didn't* do in high school – a thousand deaths.

The quote stayed with me. "A coward dies a thousand deaths; a hero but one." That cat was quoting Shakespeare, who never gets old. I see that guy's story as an example of how what you expect of yourself – and what others expect of you – influences your behaviour. The bully didn't expect this cat to get up. The bully *did* think he was a coward. And because this man – who went on to become a champion kick boxer and a successful comedian – believed the bully's expectation, he wasn't on point, he didn't get up, and he made his fear of being a coward come true.

responded at all. Months later, I got a letter that basically said, "Sorry, dude, we ain't feelin' you, but thanks." Although I was very discouraged by these rejections, I also felt a great sense of accomplishment from having taken the risk.

So even though I didn't get a label deal out of it, I went for it and I have no regrets whatsoever. All that hustle and grinding got me prepared for what the rest of life had in store for me.

Whatever you do, it's important to go full throttle. Just make sure you have a map.

<<REWIND

Taking risks helps you build confidence. If you don't succeed this time, you will learn a valuable lesson that will position you for success in the future.

Exercise 9: **Prep for Success**

1. Think of a time when you know you didn't give a task your all (job interview, live performance, audition, etc). Write down in your Vision Book how your half-stepping made you feel, especially knowing that this specific opportunity has slipped by you forever.

2. Reflect on this example and explore your motivations for not putting all your effort in. Why did you come half-assed?

3. What did you learn about yourself from this situation? What can you do the next time to mentally prepare yourself for success?

Whenever I see George, I'm reminded that it's possible to succeed in different areas without compromising your identity or integrity — and that it's possible to have a long-running career in entertainment.

He began as a DJ on Toronto's rock station, 102.1 The Edge, but I didn't meet him till years later, when he was a MuchMusic VJ in the late 90s. I knew George would have a great career in television because he is a smart cat, and he always struck me as confident and socially aware, both in terms of local and global issues.

(Only thing is, dude speaks *way* too fast. Guess all those years in radio and at MuchMusic made him aware of time and how limited it is.)

When he got his own show on CBC, *The Hour*, I was so proud of him — and inspired by him. I thought, "Damn, I want to be on that show!"

George showed me that I was on the right track by continuing to make transitions and to reinvent myself in creative and relevant ways. And that maybe if I learn to talk faster, I'll be able to get even *more* done!

Shoutout: GEORGE STROUMBOULOPOULOS

10: FALLING DOWN

"There is suffering in life, and there are
defeats. No one can avoid them. But it's better
to lose some of the battles in the struggles
for your dreams than to be defeated without
ever knowing what you're fighting for."
                                — PAULO COELHO

On Christmas Eve 1989, I did my last performance of the year at the Concert Hall in Toronto. I was opening for one of the greatest MCs of all time, Big Daddy Kane. This was when he had just released his second album, *It's a Big Daddy Thing*. He was at the peak of his career.

I still remember looking at that yellow concert flyer. Right underneath Kane's picture was mine. In hip hop, street credibility is very important. So just because I had a record deal didn't mean I had true props. And the Concert Hall was still the toughest crowd to win over. I *had* to murder this show. My goal was to do a better set than Kane – I always want to keep pushing my performance up a notch. I'd been rehearsing with my crew all week; my dancers, Frankie and Derek, known back then as Act I and Act II – the two illest b-boys in Toronto at the time – had brand-new routines just for this show, and we were tight. My DJ, LTD, was ready to kill it! By sound check, I was completely amped because I knew this was going to be the night to show my city what my crew and I were really made of. At that time, it was one of the biggest nights of my life.

All pumped, I went on and started killing my set. I was on fire – until the mics died halfway through! I kept performing, hoping the sound would come back on, but it didn't, and I couldn't take any more boos.

I was pissed off and all that positive, amped-up energy suddenly turned to anger. My blood was pumping, and as I left the stage, I heard a couple of clowns in the crowd laughing, as if they got a kick out of my show being cut short or my not being able to give a dope performance. That got me more heated.

I went into the dressing room, slammed the door, and began hurling bottles against the wall. *What the fuck? How did this happen? Did someone sabotage my show?* I had all kinds of crazy thoughts going through my mind. I was angry, but more than that, I was disappointed. I was so down that I didn't even want to watch Kane's show.

I had a plan, and despite my (and my crew's) best efforts, it didn't pan out the way I'd wanted. I started to doubt myself, to wonder if I was really ready to take my career to the next level. Under all this anger were two competing expectations: The haters expected me to fail, and I expected myself to murder the show. And when I couldn't, it hurt. I began to wonder if the haters were right. At the end of the night, still defeated, we packed up our equipment into Farley's van and drove back to Scarborough. Merry Christmas!

BTW: When You're the One Sabotaging Yourself

Be honest about where you are in terms of expectations of yourself. If at this point you don't believe you can achieve your vision – if there's a voice in the back of your head constantly criticizing you – you may wind up consciously or subconsciously doing things to screw up your plan. Maybe this has happened to you before – you've started a project and you're excited but then something has happened to derail you. Maybe it seemed like an outside force you had no control over, or maybe you're aware you did something to undercut yourself.

When something does go wrong, go ahead and get pissed or wallow for a day, or whatever you do to immediately feel better. But just for a day, at the most. Then take a hard look at what happened. Was there any way in which you were responsible? (The answer may be no, and then it isn't self-sabotage.)

If you have a pattern of sabotaging yourself, try this: sit down and have a conversation with the part of you that's undermining your success. Don't beat yourself up; just figure out what it is exactly you're afraid of. Maybe failure is more comfortable than success, so a part of you is trying to stay in your comfort zone. In that situation, remind the part of you that's sabotaging your efforts that you're aiming for an even *more* comfortable zone!

By now, you've got to know I'm a huge football fan. And this cat Chad Ochocinco is a wide receiver for the Cincinnati Bengals, and he's also one of my favourite players.

He's made the Pro Bowl five times. He's set records and then broken them. Right now, he holds at least six Bengal franchise records. He is all about having fun while being a champion – his headspace, his personality, his approach to the game. He even legally changed his last name from Johnson to Ochocinco to match his uniform number, 85 (Ochocinco in Spanish means eight five).

Then came the 2008–2009 season. My man had a very disappointing season with only 540 yards and 53 catches. (For those of you who don't know football, that's sub-par for a superstar receiver.)

Before the next season, he said, "The dreams of my future have no room for the devastations of my past – last season." He told everybody – and he's a talker, so he gets quoted a lot – that he was forgetting the bad season and ready to come back like the champion he is. He even predicted his previous full-season numbers would be matched by the fifth game, if not the fourth, of the 2009–2010 season. In the off-season he revamped his training routine, as well as his state of mind, and came back to camp ready to rock.

By the end of the 2009–2010 season, Sir Ocho had once again reached another 1,000-yard milestone and helped the Bengals win their division and reach the playoffs for the first time in ten years. He didn't let a bad season keep him down.

Most of us aren't going to have a whole bad season. We might have a bad game or three, but Chad is proof that even when things go wrong for a long period of time, it's possible to get up, dust yourself off, and get back in the game. You just have to make some adjustments and have a positive attitude.

It might have taken me a while to calm down, but I later realized that even though I had felt humiliated when my mic cut out, I can honestly say it was worth it to have had the opportunity to be on stage at all. I also thought of how many people would die to be in my position, and how blessed I am in general. This experience also made me realize that it's important in these situations, when things don't go your way, to contemplate what bigger artists would do.

It's a given that there will be pitfalls and disappointments on the path to your destination. It's inevitable. Just know that you will get through it and live another day. I chose these words intentionally, because whenever I've gone through times like that, I thought I was going to die . . . but I lived to write this book.

In times of defeat we all feel discouraged and doubt ourselves to some extent. And sometimes we think that feeling's never going to go away, but it does. We can't let that feeling take us over or allow us to lower our expectations of ourselves. To me, a true champion is someone who, when he's tackled and down flat on his face, hauls himself up, wipes the dirt off his shoulders, and gets his mind focused back on the playoffs. He doesn't let a little self-doubt get in the way.

"The dreams of my future have no room for the devastations of my past."
– Chad Ochocinco

Once I got some perspective on it, I realized that the situation at the Concert Hall – including the laughing idiots – all that comes with the territory. Doesn't matter how much I prepare, things won't always go my way or according to my plan. I also took a look at the bigger picture. Yo, I got a record deal! And years later, like, a lot of years later, I could say *I got to open for Big Daddy Kane, suckas!*

<<REWIND

Always set high expectations for yourself, but know that sometimes you won't be able to meet them, and that's okay. Aiming for greatness and hitting good is better than aiming for good and hitting average. Raise the damn bar!

Exercise 10: **Celebrate You and Yours**

1. The best time to celebrate your victories is when you're feeling down. Don't dwell on the negatives. Make a list of your small victories to date and then keep adding to it. Keep it posted somewhere you can see it, as well as in your Vision Book, so when you have a setback, you can see how much you've already accomplished and keep the problem in perspective.

2. Write a short story about your next milestone – your next gallery exhibition, your next presentation to the board, your next game, etc. Write it exactly as you want it to happen.

11: UNDER PRESSURE

*"The drama and the demands and the
pressure and all of the people giving you so
much access to so many things can be too
much. So couple that with everyone telling
you you're so this and so that and so perfect
and of course you can lose yourself."*

— BEYONCÉ KNOWLES

Sometimes, despite your best efforts and good
intentions, you're going to meet adversity, probably in several areas at once. One of the things
about success, especially in the music industry, is that
once you hit the top, some people start watching how
long it will take you to fall to the bottom again. And a
few even try to kick you there.

In mid 1992, after years of grinding in Toronto, I
packed up my stuff and moved to Brooklyn, New York. I
felt I had done all I could do in Canada; I had hit the
glass ceiling and I needed more opportunity for growth

and potential for success. Besides, the record label I had signed a deal with was in New York (I'll tell you all about how I landed it in Chapter 14).

The choice to move south was a tough one, and during the decision-making process, I had spent a lot of time reflecting on what I'd accomplished: My second album hadn't done as well as my first, although it went gold, but at least I helped out a lot of local artists by putting them on wax for the first time in their careers.

Things in New York didn't go as well as I had hoped they would.

1994 was a hard year. I released my third record, *Naaah, Dis Kid Can't Be from Canada?!!* I had some wicked tracks on it, but to say it wasn't received well in Canada would be an understatement. One of the biggest music critics back home in Toronto, Errol Nazareth, dissed it hard. Other artists were hating on it big-time. A few years earlier, I'd had the flyest LP, and had won Juno and MuchMusic Video awards. Now I felt like Shit Boy McGillicutty because people weren't feeling my music like they had in the past.

On top of all that, I was hearing that cats in Toronto weren't feeling the album title. It was frustrating because it was a real quote. That's what Red Hot Lover Tone, of super-production team Track Masters, said to me when we met. He was so impressed with my rhyme skills that when I said I was from Canada, he didn't believe me: "Naaah, you can't be from Canada." Just like a lot of the hip hop heads in New York, especially in the early 90s, he didn't expect my skills to be on such a high level.

So I thought I was making a statement that Canadian MCs are just as dope as American MCs, but some of my Canadian fans didn't get what I was trying to say.

The title was meant to show Canada some love and reinforce national pride – I was wearing a Toronto Argonauts jacket and Toronto Blue Jays cap on the cover – but some folks back home were taking it the wrong way.

The fickle T-Dot perspective was that I was dissing my city and my country. I got divinely scrutinized.

Things got tougher. I'd been going, going, going nonstop for what felt like forever. I was burned out. Maybe I tried too hard, did too much – producing 80 per cent of my record while doing all of my own college and commercial radio promotion as well as doing my own street teamwork – my mind, body, and spirit were drained.

In retrospect I now know that I should've taken a break. I can still remember all the anxiety I felt during the whole production of that album. At the time I thought I needed to just buckle down and grind. And that's what I did – I forced the album. I poured my heart and soul into that project, but by the end of it there wasn't much left of me. Looking back, I think I stretched myself too thin, and although there's no way to know for sure, I bet you the album would've been fresher if I had allowed myself the chance to step back and regroup.

Creativity and inspiration cannot be forced – they can only flow.

Creativity and inspiration cannot be forced – they can only flow. And stress and anxiety and pressure create a bottleneck effect. They plug your mind and prevent positivity and ideas from pouring out. I've experienced this enough times to be an expert on the matter. As a songwriter, and now as an author, writer's block is my enemy number-one.

When I'm feeling pressured with stress and anxiety, I find it therapeutic to take a step back and give myself some time (even if it's just a few minutes) to breathe before I move on with a project. I also find it helpful to look back at my previous work, or the work of others, for inspiration.

For example, when I'm working on some new music and I feel blocked, I will listen to a song I've already recorded or I will put on Public Enemy or Wu-Tang Clan and get amped. I'm sure to hear something that moves me or gives me that idea I was earlier hitting my head against the wall to get.

These are techniques I've found useful and you might too. It's up to you to figure out what works best for you when you're under pressure and in need of inspiration. And then do it!

Fast-forward to October of 1995. I set up a meeting with the heads of the label and said, "We're going in different directions, and we have been for a long time." We made a mutual agreement to let me out of my contract and that was that. It sounds simple, but it was a very stressful period for me. I needed a pep talk from somebody, but there was nobody I could count on. It sucked.

When the pressure is on, we really see what we're made of.

Donovan Bailey gave me hope at a very dark time in my life. In 1994, I was living in New York City, my current album wasn't doing too well, and I felt like I couldn't do anything right. So to see this brother win the title of "fastest man in the world" was a highlight in a depressing time for me. I can't express how much that inspired me. I was close to quitting music, and that one race put my head back in the game. I thought, "Nobody can rob me of this. As black Canadians, we can compete on the world stage, we can do it as well or better than anyone else . . . and we can *win*." There were a lot of parallels. And he reached his destination, too.

But that's the thing. In life we're going to have times that really test our character. I call it "Jordan in the Fourth." Michael Jordan is arguably the greatest basketball player of all time, with six NBA Championships behind him. But what he really deserves props for is this: No matter how far the point spread, when his team was down in the fourth quarter, he would take that pressure, use it as inspiration, score thirty points and clinch the win for his team. When the pressure is on, we really see what we're made of.

Remember what I said in the Preface (you might want to go back and read it if you haven't already) about the driver on my tour bus who told me to keep a baby picture of myself in my wallet? He said, "Now keep that picture in your wallet, and look at it when times get hard for you. When you look at the photo, think how far you've come since that was taken. After all this, are you going to let the negativity of your recent events prevent you from moving forward?" Hell, no!

<<REWIND

In life we're going to have times that really test us, despite our best efforts to stay on track. Sometimes this pressure might be debilitating. If it's proving too much for you to handle, take the time you need to breathe. Stepping out of the equation for a minute (but not too much time so you don't risk losing your focus or momentum) will allow you to reflect on what you've done and put things into perspective. This time may give you the space you need to map out your next move. Don't let negativity and pressure hold you back from striving to reach your destination.

Exercise 11: **The F-Word**

1. Write down three examples of a time when you thought you were going to fail but you surprised yourself and were successful.

a) _____

b) _____

c) _____

Think back to these times. Why do you think you were able to overcome the obstacles that made you doubt yourself in the first place?

a) _____

b) _____

c) _____

2. Now write down three examples of a time when you failed at something but you bounced back.

a) _____

b) _____

c) _____

What did you do during these times to help speed up the healing process?

a) _____

b) _____

c) _____

3. Scrounge up two baby pictures of yourself (or pictures you can find of you at your youngest). Paste one on the inside cover of your Vision Book and place the other in your wallet. Refer to these photos when you need a reminder of your accomplishments and how far you have come. Instant pick-me-up!

12: RESILIENCE AND PERSEVERANCE

"I never thought of losing, but now that it's happened, the only thing is to do it right. That's my obligation to all the people who believe in me. We all have to take defeats in life."
—MUHAMMAD ALI

few years ago, I had a first-thing-in-the-morning audition right after my last show of a mini-tour with D12 (Eminem's group), Joe Budden, and Royce Da 5'9". The show was on Vancouver Island, which is about eighty kilometres and a ferry ride away from downtown Vancouver, and the audition was even further away, in North Vancouver – meaning after ninety minutes on the ferry, I had another fifty kilometres or so to drive on the mainland. In order to get to the audition on time, I had to catch the 6:30 a.m. ferry.

All weekend long, my head had been in this script. Every minute I wasn't in sound check or performing, I was preparing for the audition. It was a small role but it was on a pretty big television show, so I studied hard for it. The way I saw it, whether I got the role or not, at least I'd be seeing new casting directors and producers, so I was ready to go all out.

So I made it to the audition. I had a touch of nerves hovering – my pulse was revved up, there was a little sharp pain in the back of my head, but these were normal things I usually got with anxiety. As the casting director introduced me to the director and executive producer, I relaxed a bit, and in my heart I could feel that I was about to have a wicked audition. Soon as I started, though, I heard someone coughing. I tried to ignore it and keep going. I was trying to focus on my scene, but the coughing turned into hacking. I blocked it out; I was going to show them I could focus. Then I heard the executive producer say, "Stop, stop. I'm sorry. Can you please start over? I don't know why I'm coughing like this. So sorry."

I took a deep breath and started over, only to hear the executive producer start coughing again. Now it sounded like he was hacking up a damn lung. His eyes were mad watery and his face was deep red. He stopped me again and said (in mid-cough), "I'm sorry, I don't know what's come over me. I have to leave the room." As he walked out, he joked, "Wes, I don't think you'll ever work with me."

Everyone in the room laughed, so I did too. Inside, though, I was thinking, "What's dude's problem? Is he allergic to me? Doesn't like my cologne?" It threw me off for the rest of the audition. I left the audition feeling

BTW: Junos

Be prepared for success to unfold along its own timeline. Like many things in life, you'll encounter situations that don't make sense while you're in them. Later, it might turn out that one thing that seemed like a negative led to another thing that was better than you ever could have imagined.

This is what happened to me with the Junos.

In 1990, "Backbone" was nominated for the Juno in the category of Best Dance Single. There was no Rap category. On top of that, I was asked to perform. I walked onto the stage, looked out into the auditorium full of faces, and thought, *Wow, this is like the Canadian version of the Grammys.* As I was performing "Backbone," I remembered watching Michael Jackson perform at the Grammys and wondered if this was how he felt.

That was a highlight, but less than an hour later, I got slammed down.

"The nominees in the category of Best Dance Single are . . .

"'Yada Yada,' Jam Jam Jam.

"'Missing You,' Candi.

"'I Beg Your Pardon,' Kon Kan.

"'Let Your Backbone Slide,' Maestro Fresh-Wes —"

I heard the crowd cheer for me, and Farley, who was a couple of seats down from me, leaned over and flashed me a big grin.

" — and 'Under Your Spell,' Candi."

I knew I was going to win, but still my heart was pounding so loud I could barely hear the announcement.

"And the Juno for Best Dance Single goes to . . ."

I started to get up.

"Kon Kan, for 'I Beg Your Pardon'!"

What? What the fuck? My crew looked at me, like "What happened?" Farley kept doing a double-take, like we must have heard the announcement wrong. My head was spinning. *Don't you know "Backbone" is the only Canadian hip hop song to break the Top 40?*

I was pissed. I skipped the parties and went straight home after the awards. I talked with my crew, and we figured there were politics involved, because by any other standard, we would've won for sure. I didn't know if or when I'd get another honour like this.

After a while, my bitterness turned to indifference, and I moved on. I focused all my energy onto my first full-length record, *Symphony in Effect*.

The next year, I was blown away when I found out the Junos had created a Best Rap Recording category. The album that had been my outlet for getting past the previous Juno debacle, *Symphony in Effect*, won.

If I had released the album the year before, it *wouldn't* have won, because there was no category it fit into. If "Backbone" had won, there's a chance *Symphony* might not have been eligible the next year. So you never know what might happen. One thing might look like a setback or disappointment, but could turn out better than you could ever imagine.

discouraged, really second-guessing myself. I was like, "Shit, I could have slept in and taken a later ferry back to Vancouver, instead of killing myself to get there for a half-assed audition." It really bothered me for a few days.

Things like this will always happen in life, where we get thrown for a loop and then we have to re-evaluate the situation. Then sometimes we get all crazy with it and have thoughts like, "Was his coughing a sign that I'm in the wrong profession?" "Was he serious when he said,

There's always light at the end of the tunnel. I just wish sometimes that the tunnel wasn't so damn long.

'We'll never work together'?" We're all going to face adversity and have setbacks but the important thing is to keep going. There's always light at the end of the tunnel. I just wish sometimes that the tunnel wasn't so damn long.

Once I calmed down, I realized, yeah, it was a sign – a sign that the role wasn't right for me. Eventually I was able to see that something good came out of it – at least new producers and casting directors saw me. And hopefully I would get a call for another audition, totally unrelated to this executive producer – someone who might be allergic to me.

How to Win the War

Some of us keep getting down on ourselves when we screw up, and that stops us from getting up again. If you can put it behind you and just move forward, you'll feel better because you're moving on to success, and because you didn't stay stuck in the negative mindset.

Here are a few words (of wisdom) to keep in mind:

- It's really important to remember that you don't have to win every battle. Just win the war.
- The only thing you can control are your own actions. You can't predict anyone's reaction or anything external. It's all beyond you.

- It's not pessimism to acknowledge that sooner or later, something's going to go wrong. It's not a matter of "if" but of "when." Just know that it happens to everybody. And when it does happen, we all feel discouraged and doubt ourselves to some degree. Sometimes it seems like that feeling's never going to go away, but it does. Trust me.

No Matter What, Keep Doing Your Thing

Director Gail Harvey nearly traumatized me as an actor. I almost wanted to quit because of her (she's going to laugh when she reads this).

It was back in the days when I did a TV series called *Metropia*. We shot ninety episodes in ninety days, which is gruelling for any actor to do, much less a rookie, like I was then. It was acting boot camp. The producers kept bringing Gail back to direct more episodes because she could deliver at this pace and make sure we didn't go into overtime – but she was a pain for me. There were times when I felt my work was wack, but Gail, man, she'd pull me aside every day to give me some brutal constructive criticism and I swear it felt like she was being mean and singling me out. I thought I'd never get another acting gig again. Looking back, I can see that it was tough love. She saw I had talent and thought I wasn't working to my full potential. It's like when a basketball or football coach is hard on you, because they know you can do better. Their criticism makes you work even harder. Believe me, there were times I wanted to walk off set, but I knew that would burn my bridges with this director, and maybe with other industry people, so I bit my tongue – and it turned out to be a very smart decision, as you'll read later.

Still, I needed support then, to balance out the criticism and to keep me encouraged, and I didn't get it. It sucks to think you've failed or you're not good enough, or your employer/coach/friend isn't giving you the love you need. Those are the times that truly test you. You have to take a deep breath and then tap into yourself for answers. After all, people can pep talk you till they've run out of words, but you're the one who's got to get up and keep going.

Here are some things that can help you during these times:

1. Remember all the sacrifices you made to get to this level.
2. Ask yourself, "Am I really going to let this person/situation get the better of me?"
3. Identify the things you learned from this experience that you can use next time.

<<REWIND

You just have to keep going in spite of adversity and setbacks, because they're inevitable. You won't win every time you step out of the gate, but you can and will succeed overall.

Exercise 12: **Dust Off Your Shoulders**

There are things you can do to help you dust off your shoulders after a defeat and get going again.

1. **Write down your blessings in your Vision Book.** We all have so much to be thankful for – friends, family, opportunities, health . . . If you can't come up with anything, then at least realize it's a blessing that you're here now and you have the opportunity to read this book. It's ideal to keep a list of your blessings every day because, over time, you'll see how they add up. Once you start looking for them, you'll be amazed how many you find.

2. **What went right?** Even when something goes monumentally wrong – a job interview, a date, a speech you're giving – there are going to be some elements of it that went right. Remember my Big Daddy Kane show disaster? I was so angry, but once I cooled down, I realized, "At least I had the opportunity to open for him. That's dope! And before the audio was switched off, the show was wicked!" Write down everything that went right, no matter how small. This will prevent you from all-or-nothing thinking and boost your self-confidence so that you can get back in the game.

3. **What Would Michael Jordan Do (WWMJD)?** How would Michael Jordan handle your situation? It doesn't have to be Michael Jordan; it can

be anyone you respect, who you think has grace under pressure. Your mother. Your brother. Your best friend. What do you think they would do in this situation?

4. **What can you learn from this?** Most of the time, there will be something you can learn from whatever went wrong. It might be that a given job isn't right for you, or that you have to further develop a particular skill.

5. **Keep your game face on.** This will do two things for you:

a) By "acting as if" you feel good and positive, you can trick your brain to think that it really does feel good and positive. How you act is how you feel. I'll get more into this later.

b) It'll show your rivals and critics that they're not affecting you. Now, it might get you down for a while – that's normal – but you don't have to let them see you down. That's what they want, and you have the opportunity to deprive them of that pleasure.

6. **Put on your flyest outfit.** This might sound superficial but there is nothing like putting on your best shirt or dress or whatever and thinking, "Damn, I look good!" This is an instant pick-me-up. But it's only temporary, so make sure you do items 1 through 5 too!

My man Kardinal Offishall is an example of Canadian hip hop artists being just as good as or better than most. His albums have always been tight and I've bought every CD he's put out.

He has made (and continues to make) a major impact worldwide; his song "Dangerous" broke the *Billboard* 100's Top 10 in 2008 – a first for a Canadian MC. He's got one of the sickest live shows I've ever seen and it makes me want to improve my own show.

And while some might say I passed the torch to him, in a literal sense, he passed it to me.

I was on stage with him one night doing a show, and he brought out – you guessed it – torches. Real, lit torches. And he passed one to me, instead of the other way around.

The point is, there is symbolism there. We have a mutual respect, and he continues to inspire me to work harder and reach further.

13: MAKE OPPORTUNITIES. NOW.

*"Don't wait for extraordinary opportunities.
Seize common occasions and make them
great. Weak men wait for opportunities;
strong men make them."*
— ORISON SWETT MARDEN

Before I had a record deal, I knew that having a video on MuchMusic would give me national exposure and help me land a contract. I decided to make my own indie music video for "I'm Showin' You." I saved up two thousand dollars from my job as a security guard at Parkway Plaza, and Farley Flex's mother co-signed a loan for another three thousand.

Now, five thousand dollars is not a lot of money for a music video budget, and it definitely couldn't get you as far then as it can today, but it was all I had, so that's what I worked with. I was nineteen, and all I knew was that I wasn't going to wait for an opportunity; I was going to make one. We shot the video at my old high school, L'Amoreaux Collegiate, which saved us

**All I knew was that
I wasn't going to wait
for an opportunity.
I was going to make one.**

money – and I knew it would grab people's attention.

The video was weak (it looks even worse now, because it's over twenty years old!). I was inexperienced and knew nothing about making videos. Plus, how much can you really do with such a small budget? What's dope about it though is that I made it happen . . . and MuchMusic put it on light rotation, which helped me start to get national exposure for the first time in my career.

I wasn't waiting for something to happen. I was being proactive. At the time I don't know that I intentionally set out to create my own opportunity. It was more that there weren't any *obvious* opportunities in front of me – I mean, there were no hip hop record companies in Canada – and I wasn't willing to sit around like a dick twiddling my thumbs. So I was creative and I came up with a way to promote myself and my music on a national platform. I knew I needed exposure and that was the best way I could think to get it.

Today we have the Internet, YouTube, satellite TV and radio – there are a lot more means to get your stuff out there. I mean, even if you're not a musician or actor, think of the possibilities. You can create your own Web site and sell your products and services directly. You can film your own commercial on your camera phone and post it on YouTube or Facebook. You can "tweet" and promote your upcoming art exhibit. I'm sure there will be a million more online tools by the time this book comes out. The possibilities are endless and growing each day.

My homies, Jessy and Ulysses Terrero, started a casting company, T&T Casting, back in the early 90s. They supervised extras casting for low-budget films. They worked with some of the hottest talent out there and developed relationships with actors, recording artists, producers, and directors and built up their database with contacts.

They used all the lessons they had learned from working in casting on various projects, as well as the contacts they had developed, to branch out and start directing music videos. Their first project was a video called "E-Z On Tha Motion" by Juno Award–winning hip hop group Ghetto Concept. They kept grinding and then Jessy got his big break – a Jill Scott video called "Gettin' in the Way." That just put him over the top and in high demand. The next thing you know, Jessy is one of the most respected and in-demand music video directors out there, with numerous MTV VMA (Video Music Awards) and *Billboard Magazine* award nominations. Between the two of them, Uly and Jessy have casted and directed, respectively, more than ten 50 Cent and G-Unit videos, not to mention videos for LL Cool J, Akon, Leona Lewis, Sean Paul, and Mary J. Blige. And they don't stop there. At the time I'm writing this, Jessy is in post-production on a film he just directed, called *Brooklyn to Manhattan* – his directorial debut was a movie called *Soul Plane*. Ulysses just finished casting his fifth music video for Jennifer Lopez. I'm very proud of those cats for making their own opportunities and creating their own empire.

The Lost Art of Bartering

If you're like me and not so technologically advanced, you need to find someone who is. There used to be a time where you had to go to school to learn about computers and creating Web sites and those types of things, but now a lot of people are self-taught and even doing it just for fun. So you don't necessarily need to find a university-educated homie with a computer science degree. Talk to your co-workers or neighbours or teammates. Hey, why not post a request on Facebook or Twitter or Craigslist for someone with these skills?

I know people charge an arm-and-a-leg for these types of services but here's the beauty: you're going to barter. Never heard that word before? I'm not surprised. It's a lost art, but one we definitely need to bring back, especially these days with so many people hit by the economic crisis. Bartering is the act of trading or swapping goods or services. Kijiji and Craigslist have pages of ads from people who are looking to trade things. You'll find fledgling photographers willing to offer their services, along with the digital images they take, in exchange for permission to use the photos to build their portfolio or Web site (here's an idea for all the aspiring photographers reading this book). People trade furniture and accessories from their houses. There are clothing swaps. I've even read about this thing called "couch-surfing" where travellers connect with hosts at their travel destination and crash on their couch – for free. It's like I said in one of my lines as Andre in *The Line*, "Now what we have here is the possibility for something called synergy." So you can see there are millions of people out there willing to share and exchange. And if you can't find someone in your community, look to the World Wide Web. In other words, you've got to be able to finagle.

I've always bartered. And no, I didn't rap for my food. A film producer/director named Andrew Burrows-Trotman stepped to me because he wanted to cast me for a role in a short film he was producing called *Amma*. He was telling me how it was coming together; he mentioned he needed a hospital to shoot a specific scene and that he was also still trying to find investors to help him finance the building of a set and the rental of a location.

Lightbulbs started flashing in my head. *Hey, I know people who could help him out with his location.* Andrew and I came to an agreement that if I helped secure some locations, I would get an executive producer credit. At the time I was working on *Instant Star* and I had a great relationship with the production company, Epitome Pictures. So I pulled in a favour from them and worked it out so **You've got to be able to finagle.** that *Amma* could be filmed on a Saturday afternoon at Epitome's production studio when they were not filming *Instant Star* or *Degrassi*. So instead of spending five thousand dollars to film in a hospital, we filmed at Epitome Pictures at no charge, except for some hospital-type props and insurance.

I also had a relationship with the set director of *Metropia*, Paul Swayze, so I called in another favour and had him build a set for the fraction of the price it would've cost if Andrew had contracted out.

That was some creative bartering, if I do say so myself. See, I didn't even directly provide the location, but I acted as a production coordinator – and that's worth something. Instead of just another acting credit, I hustled and got myself an executive producer credit. Be resourceful and figure out how you can create your own opportunities.

<<REWIND

Don't wait for opportunities to come knocking – be resourceful and create your own. Team up with people and exchange products or services.

Exercise 13: **Opportunities and You**

1. What are three things you can do *right now* to create your next opportunity?

a) _____

b) _____

c) _____

2. What kind of help do you need that can create opportunities for you in the area of promotion? What can you offer in exchange for these goods or services?

a) _____

b) _____

c) _____

14: NETWORKING

"Networking has emerged as a respected business and career skill."
— ANNE BABER AND LYNNE WAYMON

One of the most important things you can do to put your vision into action is to network. I think the word "networking" intimidates a lot of people but all it means is meeting people. In hip hop terms, "networking" is called "politicking" or "polying." It's necessary to "get your poly on" and exchange information with others. Whether you feel like it or not, you should get out there and make connections, because you never know where one of those contacts might lead.

My whole career has been established and maintained through networking – with music producers, music video and film and television directors, other celebrities and people involved in the entertainment business. I'll be honest with you, if I had sat back and been passive about moving my career to the next level – if

I hadn't networked on my own – nobody would have ever heard of me, much less remembered me. I can't stress enough how important it is to get out there, especially when you're just starting out.

From the very beginning, I've been seriously pro-active about meeting people and making sure they know my name. Talent is not good enough when there are people out there just as talented but hungrier than you, because they're willing to do more networking and self-promotion than you are. Trust me.

Plenty of times, I feel like I'm too tired to go to an event, or I wonder if it's just going to be a waste of time, and a waste of business cards. Even when I'm at some conference or party or whatever, I sometimes think, *Why should I give her a business card?* Then I have to remind myself: networking will pay off. You don't know how and you don't know when, but it will.

Remember: talent isn't good enough. The ability to network and develop relationships is priceless – and it's something you can teach yourself.

Get Out There

It was 1988 and it had been a year and a half since I took a "leave of absence" from university. Even though I was doing all right in Toronto, I was getting frustrated with trying to land a record deal.

Electric Circus was a live dance show on MuchMusic, and every week, artists would perform while dancers . . . danced. Performing on *EC* was a quick way to get local and national exposure, so when they asked me to appear, I did. I performed a song called "Can't Stop Us Now" and I *killed* it!

The *EC* producers liked me so much that right after the show, they called to book me again. At first I wasn't sure it was a good idea – been there, done that, didn't land me a record contract. Plus, my video for "I'm Showin' You" was already getting airplay on MuchMusic, so doing *EC* again seemed like it might be a step backwards, or at the least a waste of time.

Talent isn't good enough. The ability to network and develop relationships is priceless – and it's something you can teach yourself.

But Farley convinced me that it would be a good move so I booked a date to return and perform "Backbone" – the first time I would perform it live. I decided I'd try out the tuxedo concept and see how it went over.

The night of the performance came, and I was not feeling it; I didn't want to do *Electric Circus* again. I was anxious – anxiety-attack anxious, complete with stabbing pain at the base of my skull – and frustrated. *Maybe I'm not good enough. Maybe the naysayers are right and my career isn't going anywhere. Maybe I'm exaggerating by calling it a "career."*

My anxiety was building. *Maybe I'd never get a deal.* I'd been rhyming since I was a kid, and my career hadn't popped off yet. *Maybe I should throw in the towel, go back to university and do what I'm* supposed *to do.*

Even though these fears were racing through my mind, I managed to push them to the back and focus on how amped I'd feel after a dope performance.

And yeah, I killed it again, but the best thing about that night was that dance music artist Stevie B was also performing on *EC*. I didn't even notice him watching my performance, but it's a good thing I got off my ass that night and went, because Stevie B hooked me up with his label folks at LMR Records in New York, and my whole life changed.

If Farley hadn't talked me into performing again, I wouldn't have been there and had the chance to meet

BTW: Allow Me to Reintroduce Myself . . .

In the summer of 1990, I went to New York City for the annual New Music Seminar, a dope networking conference where I always met a lot of people and made tons of connections. This year I met an editor of *The Village Voice* newspaper named Harry Allen. (Public Enemy dubbed him "The Media Assassin" in their hit song "Don't Believe the Hype.") We spoke briefly and that was the end of that.

The following year I returned to the seminar and ran into Harry again. I recognized him, so I went over and reintroduced myself. He told me that although he remembered my face, he was glad I had introduced myself again because he met a lot of people at these events. He said that he actually learned from Salt, of the female rap group Salt-N-Pepa, the value of reintroducing yourself to someone in a networking environment. She had explained to him you shouldn't assume people remember you, and that even if they remember your face, they may have forgotten your name but may be too embarrassed to ask it.

Do yourself a favour and make sure people know your name.

and poly with Stevie B, and I wouldn't have gotten my record deal.

The main point is that it is important to not overlook opportunities to "poly" or showcase your stuff, because they play out when you least expect it. I'm living proof of that. *Electric Circus* was a great place for my networking. Every time I drive in downtown Toronto along Queen Street West and look at that building, I think to myself, "This is where it all started. This is where my life changed." And to think, I almost threw away the opportunity because I didn't "feel like it."

When you know you should get out there and meet people, but you don't feel like it, come back and re-read this story.

Get Closer

It's a strange job that requires me to beat up a co-worker on the first day. That's how it was with *The Line*, though – we shot a scene where I had to rough up one of the lead actors, Clé Bennett. As a "getting to know you" situation, it didn't create great vibes.

So I took Clé out for a drink after work. It was the least I could do after shoving him around and bruising him up all day.

I let him know where I was coming from and told him I was there to murder the show. I said straight up that I would always come prepared, and that I'd be open to working

It is important to not overlook opportunities to "poly" or showcase your stuff, because they play out when you least expect it.

with him to find different ways to make our scenes even better than they already were.

Once we chopped it up outside our working environment, we became good friends. Developing relationships can always help in building the positive energy (or breaking down the negative energy) that people may show towards you when they first meet you.

Get to Conferences

In 1998, I went to a music seminar in Montreal. On my flight, the passenger sitting next to me was a young, up-and-coming entertainment lawyer named Chris Taylor. By the time we landed in Montreal, Chris and I had really made a good connection. I felt that we could work together one day and perhaps I'd hire him to negotiate my next record deal.

When we got to the conference, I went to one of the panels where I heard a lawyer by the name of Susan Abramovitch speak. She mentioned the artists on her roster, and one of them was Randy Bachman. A lightbulb went off in my head. I hadn't yet received permission for the sample from Randy's (and Burton Cummings') song "These Eyes" for my song "Stick to Your Vision." To make a long story short, I exchanged information with Susan and hired her to negotiate my new record deal with Attic Records, as well as to help me get the permission and sample clearance for "These Eyes."

Although I'd made a good connection with Chris Taylor, Susan was the right person to represent me on this specific project. I have worked with Chris on other projects since that one, but in that instance, it made the most sense to go with Susan given her affiliation with Randy Bachman.

If I hadn't gone to the conference, I wouldn't have met either one of them. But because I did, I developed two new contacts, and I have ended up working with both of them.

Get a Leg Up

Networking is important in any industry. That old cliché, "It's not *what* you know but *who* you know" (and who knows you) is as true for actors and musicians as it is for business people or writers. Sometimes, the only way to stand out from the other five hundred resumés or audition tapes is to have someone refer you.

In 1999, I was asked to write a song for the film score of *The Hurricane*, a Hollywood film based on the life of the boxer Rubin "Hurricane" Carter, who was wrongly imprisoned for murder. I was really excited, because

During my trip to New York City in the summer of 1990 for the annual New Music Seminar, I saw this new upcoming female MC hit the stage at one of the showcases. She was rolling pretty deep as well – backed by the Jungle Brothers, and Afrika Bambaataa. Her name was Queen Latifah, though on stage the Jungle Brothers gave her the title "Momma Zulu." She walked onto that stage with mad confidence. I'll never forget it. She rhymed over some sick beats produced by DJ Mark the 45 King and her voice was commanding and powerful. It's been amazing to watch her evolve in so many different ways throughout the years. She continued to develop relationships in not only the music industry but in the film and television industry as well. By using hip hop as her launching pad, she has taken off and is now a true conglomerate. She runs her own production company, Flavor Unit; has starred in two TV series and many movies (including her Oscar-nominated performance in *Chicago*); she's the face of CoverGirl cosmetics; she does voice work in animations . . . Queen Latifah defines dope.

She inspired me to keep it moving and to not be restricted by the parameters of hip hop culture. She was and is strong enough to establish and enforce her presence as a female MC in this male-dominated industry; beyond that, she's creative and ambitious enough to continually reinvent herself in different fields and roles. I have the utmost respect for her.

the people who asked me to contribute were the ones the movie was based on, the actual people who tried to get Hurricane out of prison. Terry Swinton, Lisa Peters, and Sam Chaiton were fans of my song "Stick to Your Vision" and wanted something similar that was inspirational and evoked emotion. So I watched a rough cut of the movie and wrote a song called "Perseverance." The chorus of the song was inspired by the last words Hurricane said while behind bars, which were, "Hate got me in here, but love's going to get me out." Long story short, it didn't happen – my song didn't make the score, or even the soundtrack. That was a big disappointment for me, and I was upset for a while. I felt the opportunity could've helped my career.

The Hurricane came out in 2000. Four years later, I landed a part in *Redemption: The Stan Tookie Williams Story*. My audition was good, but the main reason I got the part is that the executive producer of the movie, Rudy Langlais, was also the executive producer of *The Hurricane* – and he'd liked the track "Perseverance" and remembered me.

I guess it's true that when one door closes, another one opens.

<<REWIND
The key to networking is to *just do it* – everywhere you can. It doesn't matter if you don't want to, and it doesn't matter if you don't know how, it will pay off – someday, somehow, and often better than you ever could have imagined.

Exercise 14: **Get Your "Poly" On**

1. Below, list three networking events you could attend in the next few months. If there are no events, list alternate ways you'll reach out and meet people (such as answering questions on LinkedIn).

a) _____

b) _____

c) _____

2. First impressions are important so think of what type of impact you'd like to make from the jump-off. Use the spaces below to brainstorm on what tools you will need (for example, business cards or flyers), how you will start a conversation (such as by complimenting the other person, talking about a current event that could segue into your skills or services), and what you will wear during networking opportunities (for instance, is a suit appropriate attire?).

a) _____

b) _____

c) _____

15: BUILDING YOUR TEAM

"I can't stress enough the importance of surrounding yourself with energy that supports your goals."

— KANYE WEST

To realize your vision, you have to have the right tools, and that includes having the right people around you. If people you normally roll with are not elevating you – pushing you to reach higher and celebrating your achievements – they are stunting your growth. Get them out of your life.

I always heard there's strength in numbers and that there's no such thing as a one-man army. And I have to admit that I have always had a problem letting other people do work for me. In music, film, television, and anything else I've done, I've always gotten my hands dirty. Even on the music tip, when I first came out, Farley Flex didn't exactly "manage" me. It was the two of us managing – or attempting to manage – me.

Everything from song ideas to radio promotion, video concepts, etc. – I have always had to be involved. Maybe if I'd truly trusted a team to work with me and on my behalf, I could've gone farther in terms of touring and getting known globally, like my man Kardinal Offishall is doing now or like Dream Warriors did when they went platinum in the U.K. back in the 90s.

The point is, regardless of your profession – whether you're a pastor, a student, an architect, or a musician – you can always benefit from having the right people around you. Like my homie/producer, Jay Rome, always says, "As dope as Michael Jordan was (as a basketball player), he never passed the ball to himself."

At the very least, everybody needs love. We all need people around us who support us and cheer us on, who can help us up when we fall and celebrate with us when we achieve a milestone.

In a practical sense, a team of people can get more done than any one individual can. Four hands are better than two, and ten are even better than four. By surrounding yourself with people whose strengths complement your own and who are willing to help, you can make yourself that much more of a contender. This truth was definitely reinforced in my mind during the whole process of creating this book. I mean, sure, I'd been conceptualizing it for the last four or five years, but I ain't no Margaret Atwood or Ernest Hemingway. I enlisted

> We all need people around us who support us and cheer us on, who can help us when we fall and celebrate with us when we achieve a milestone.

Mike Tomlin, coach of the 2009 Super Bowl–winning Pittsburgh Steelers, inspires me to be a better, more responsible leader and reminds me of the importance of developing a team. Mike is the youngest coach to ever bring his team to the Super Bowl and only the second African-American coach to win it.

He began his career as an assistant defensive back coach, and through hard work, he became head coach; now he can lay claim to motivating world champions. I am inspired by Coach Tomlin's drive and his ability to lead individuals to move together as a team towards a specific goal.

---

a whole bunch of people to help get it done. I talked to all the published authors I know to figure out how to get a book deal, or to see if I should just self-publish. Once I determined I didn't want to self-publish my book, I went through my network to see if I could get a meeting with a publisher – it just so happened my friend Terry Markus knew someone at McClelland & Stewart – all this before I had even finished the first draft of the book. Not to mention all the help I got during the writing process from my wife, Tamara, or all the editing of the manuscript from my editor, Liz, and the copy editor, Lynn.

It's very important to remember that you would not be able to have the same level of success without your team's contributions. Like I always say, you can be the greatest quarterback in the League, but if you're not on the right team, you ain't going to the Super Bowl.

What if you're guilty, like me most times, of being a lonely soldier? Maybe it's by choice, and maybe it isn't, but just think how much further you could go if you had someone helping you. I know the idea of loosening the reins is kind of scary, but there are actions you can take to build yourself a team.

Finding a Mentor

One way to improve is to hang out with someone who has more experience – and more success – in your field than you do.

I wish there had been other artists to guide me when I was starting out in music. That was back when Canadian hip hop was in its infancy and there wasn't anybody who was able to school me, but when I got into TV and film acting, I found a few people to give me advice along the way. Some are even younger than I am, like my man K. C. Collins, whom I've worked with on several projects (if you don't know who he is, check out *Owning Mahowny*, with Academy Award–winner Philip Seymour Hoffman, or *Poor Boy's Game*, in which he played Danny Glover's son). He may be a few years younger than I am, but any time I need advice, K.C. makes time to show me what he knows. I have him to thank for giving me insight

> Like I always say, you can be the greatest quarterback in the League, but if you're not on the right team, you ain't going to the Super Bowl.

into agents, managers, and the overall acting scene in Los Angeles.

In 2001, we did a movie together called *Conviction*. I was amped, because I had a scene with Omar Epps. The day we wrapped filming I was anxious to see the thing, so I went to K.C. and asked, "When do you think the movie's going to come out?"

He looked at me and chuckled. "Wes, what you gotta learn is that after you finish a film, it ain't gonna come out for another year or so. Just forget about this one for now and keep it moving."

Damn, he's right. I'd thought I was going to be getting my shine on sooner than that, but he had a good point: Go after the next one, make it even better than this one.

Once you complete a project, it's important to set your sights on the next mission. Or as my actor-friend, Clé Bennett, would say, "If you know you murdered it, you got no business hanging around the scene of the crime." Look forward, not backward. If K.C. hadn't told me to keep it moving, I might've waited a long time and become frustrated, bored, or discouraged. Don't be afraid to ask questions. Mentors can help you avoid certain pitfalls that they themselves met along the way.

<<REWIND

You benefit from surrounding yourself with the "right" people – they can keep you sharp. You need people around you not only to give support and encouragement along the way buy also to help you celebrate your victories.

Exercise 15: **Create Your Crew**

1. What can your team do to help make you feel more confident? Think about the times you've felt most amped and figure out what exactly made you feel that way. Was it getting a pep talk from your partner? Getting your blood pumping with an early-morning workout with a friend? Make sure you know what makes you feel your best – both what you do yourself and what other people say or do to support you. Make sure the people close to you know that if you're discouraged, the best thing they can do is, say, go for a run with you – not bring you a pint of ice cream (unless that's what works for you). Get out your Vision Book and brainstorm – write down anything and everything that comes to mind.

2. What are your weak points? Do you need help with time management? Getting out of bed in the morning (or making yourself go to bed at night)? Maybe you love learning but aren't the world's most efficient researcher? Make a list in your Vision Book and write down everything that comes to mind. This list shows you where you need help.

3. Now write a list of people who are strong in the areas where you are weak. Then go ahead and ask them for help. Don't be shy!

16: DIFFERENTIATE YOURSELF

"It's the way you play that makes it. Play like
you play. Play like you think, and then you
got it, if you're going to get it. And whatever
you get, that's you . . . that's your story."
— Count Basie

often hear many old school music critics dismiss this
generation of artists as unimaginative, but I have to
say that Kanye West is one of the most creative artists I've heard in a while. "Jesus Walks," from his debut
album, was a brave single to release, especially in an
era when it's cool to seem stupid. He also came up
with a dope concept by creating a college-based theme
for his first three albums: *The College Dropout, Late
Registration,* and *Graduation.* The trilogy tells a whole
story. Not too many artists take the time, or energy, to
make albums so conceptual.

Even his later albums show growth and that he's not
afraid to push the envelope.

It's important to try to push yourself to see how great you can be. Surprise yourself and challenge your own creativity . . . otherwise you're simply robbing yourself of your potential. Tapping into yourself, digging deep and extracting your true thoughts, ideas, and feelings, is elevation, because it proves what you're made of and highlights your uniqueness. It's growth.

The Maestro Concept

It's essential to make yourself stand out from other people. Even if you're the best, there's a saying that "everybody needs a hook" – something to catch other people, to make them pay attention, so that *then* they'll see how wicked you are.

You can take something that's part of your personality, appearance, or life (like Kanye's "College" concept), or you can look at what's already been done and choose something different. Ideas are everywhere.

When I started out, I was "Melody MC" and after that I was known as "Fresh-Wes." People told me I had to add something to that moniker, but I didn't know what. During the "Fresh-Wes" days, I was working as a security guard at a mall in Toronto, and every day I walked by a store called Tuxedo Royale. One day I thought, "That's dope." I decided to bring a classical vibe to the "Fresh-Wes" idea. That's where the Maestro concept originated.

After I came up with the Maestro theme, I started thinking about my approach. I knew I didn't want my first album to be just a bunch of songs slapped together like a compilation record. I'd been listening to a lot of Public Enemy, and from them I'd learned that an album has to be conceptualized top to bottom if you want to stand out. In keeping with the Maestro idea, I decided to call the album *Symphony in Effect*. From beginning to end, *Symphony in Effect* was constructed strategically and conceptually. Everything grew out of the classical idea: Side A was First Concerto and Side B was Second Concerto. But don't get the wrong idea, it was definitely a hip hop album, and it had major influences from Public Enemy's and Marley Marl's production styles.

The album ended with an instrumental track titled "Fortissimo," which is a music term meaning very loud, abbreviated as *ff*. Throughout the album, I made references to classical music terms. For example, in "Backbone" I said, "This ain't Forte [loud]. I'm coming double F . . . Fortissimo." And I then changed the meaning, so FF stood for Funky Fresh. So even though the theme was integrating classical terms into hip hop, I made sure it would appeal to hip hop fans. Because I had a unique concept, and because I kept reinforcing it, the album stood out from other hip hop albums and is still, to this day, deemed a classic.

Staying Fresh

It's important to keep trying new ways of doing things. Switching it up keeps your mind and your focus sharp. Hold yourself to the same high standard as you do with anything else – always strive to be the best.

BTW: Dream Warriors

In 1990, when the Dream Warriors first came out, I was like, "What the hell are they smoking?" I mean, their swag was hip hop, but the song titles, like "Wash Your Face in My Sink" and "Do Not Feed the Alligators," and all that Dungeons & Dragons shit, was buggin' me out.

The group's lead MC, King Lou, was my dude, especially since we were both from T.O., but I thought initially that they were really far out. I know *I* came out with a different concept with "Maestro" and the black tux and all, but I thought the Bedknobs & Broomsticks these cats were spittin' about was really left field. Their beats were so abstract and alternative — even before the term "alternative" was really accepted in hip hop.

The more I got to know Lou, the more I realized how passionate he was about his sound — musically, lyrically, and conceptually. He was so into originality that he created his own word syncopations and rhyme styles. Biting, or copying, was not allowed.

Lou's originality in a time when hip hop was just starting to define itself might have been too risky and may have negatively impacted Dream Warriors' popularity in the U.S., but they were the first Canadian hip hop group to have a platinum LP in the U.K. That's still huge to me!

Because they refused to let anyone's expectations of hip hop define them, the Dream Warriors made not only distinctive records, but also a major contribution to the music industry. Their style was brave and innovative.

So I have to commend them for sticking to their guns, keeping it original, and making some classic hip hop. They were confident enough to be seriously original and to not let the then-current conventions of hip hop define them.

In 1984, after feeling established as a local MC, I decided to try something different. The concept of two MCs rapping off each other was something I had always wanted to try. Run-D.M.C. was starting to get popular,

Switching it up keeps your mind and your focus sharp.

and the way Run and D.M.C. knew each others' rhymes meant they were well rehearsed. No matter where one of them went lyrically, the other could match it. That's how tight they were.

I teamed up with my homie Marlon Bruce. We decided to name our group Vision (coincidental, huh?), because he thought one-word names, like Whodini, sounded cool. I gave him the name Ebony MC, and we started writing rhymes over the phone. Then we started to do our routines on CKLN, the same radio station where I got my first break.

One day, we heard a concert promoter was looking for a rap group to open for American rappers UTFO, and we sent in a demo. So did thirty-five other crews. The promoter picked the top eight and decided to have a contest to decide the winner (this was twenty years before any *Idol* show). Marlon and I asked my old DJ, Greg, to spin for us; he was also spinning for another MC earlier in the lineup, so he'd already be set up.

The night of the contest, right before Marlon and I were about to go on, Greg found us and said, "Sorry, man, I can't spin for you."

What? Marlon and I looked at each other.

"What's up?" I asked him, trying to look calmer than I felt inside.

"I screwed up spinning for that cat Sugar C, and I don't want to mess up your set, too."

I was pissed. All the practice, everything we'd done to get here, and my DJ has cold feet? Greg offered to get us another DJ, and he found a brother named DJ Howard Hughes.

> **It's important to surprise yourself and challenge your own creativity ... otherwise you're simply robbing yourself of your potential.**

I remember before we went on stage, Howard was setting up, and all I could hear was people in the crowd laughing. "Howard's DJing? *Howard?* That's a joke!" I guess you could say he didn't have the same reputation as a DJ that Greg had. That got me even angrier. Plus, Marlon was thrown off by the DJ switch, so I was trying to calm him down. This was not how I'd pictured this night going down.

I told Marlon, "We've come this far. Let's just go out there and kill it." I roared onto that stage, all my anger channelled into murdering this set. When I introduced my name as Melody MC, the crowd made noise, and I knew we had them in our hands. Hearing somebody yell, "They better fuckin' win it!" just made it sweeter.

Because Marlon and I expected a lot of ourselves – aimed to be as tight as Run-DMC – we were able to adjust to something unexpected.

And we won the contest. Our style, preparation, and execution were key.

What did we win? Sixty dollars each and two JVC radios. The prizes weren't the point. That we worked

I remember rolling with Russell Peters back in the late 90s. He was a fan of mine from day one and I've been a fan of his from the first time I saw him perform. This cat was always a joker, and he does some of the most accurate accents I've ever heard. Now, I've seen tons of comedians perform, but what makes Russell stand out is his awareness of both his own South Asian heritage and the ethnic diversity in Toronto. Because of this, he can get away with a lot more than most comedians would. (He also has more material to work with, given the city's multiculturalism!) Although Russell evolved from being a local Toronto comic to an international comedian, it's great to see him still come back to Canada and be true to his roots. My man went from performing at local night clubs to selling out stadiums and that inspires me. And the fact that he recently made the *Forbes* list as one of the wealthiest comedians? Hell, yeah! That inspires me as well.

On a more serious note, Russell's creativity is inspiring because he found something that is unique about himself and he ran with it . . . all the way to the bank. Instead of dwelling in mediocrity, he came up with an innovative concept and cornered his own market.

hard and set out to be the best and came with a fresh new concept and were able to adapt when things went wrong – that's what was important. That's what made me feel good. Plus, I had kind of reinvented myself – as one half of a duo – and I hit the local scene from a different angle.

It's too easy to become complacent when you've already established yourself or carved out your niche. That's why you need to stay fresh – to move forward and not get left behind the times. It's also a great way to expand your target market or audience. Madonna is a great example of an artist who has changed it up through the span of her career and not only kept her fans on the edge of their toes but also converted some non-believers with her ingenuity.

<<REWIND

Come up with an angle or a signature to differentiate yourself from the crowd. Remember to keep it fresh by coming up with new concepts and reinventing your brand. This will keep your audience or customers interested, as well as keep you sharp and on point.

Exercise 16: **What's Your Signature?**

Write down what makes you stand out from your competition. How can you turn this into your signature statement or part of your brand? Hint: If you can't think of anything that stands out, maybe you need to create something.

17: **PREPARATION**

*"I believe success is preparation, because
opportunity is going to knock on your door
sooner or later but are you prepared to
answer that?"*

— OMAR EPPS

In order to keep moving forward with your vision, you
need to be prepared. In order to be prepared, you need
self-discipline. And self-discipline is hard; it's enforcing
rules on yourself to act or behave a certain way. It's holding yourself up to a certain standard and kicking your own
ass when you get out of line. I find that I get better results
when I have a solid routine. A routine provides structure in your day and that's necessary to avoid getting overwhelmed by a long to-do list. I know the idea of routine
sounds boring and if you're like me, you want some variety
in your day, but I'm telling you, routine doesn't have to be
monotonous. All it's really about is helping you develop
good habits and using it as a way to combat distraction.

For me, I'm my best when I get up at about 5:30 a.m. and hit the gym. Working out gives me energy for the rest of the day and it gives me the momentum I need to stay focused. Now that I have a son, it's a challenge to hit the gym early, because I'm helping my wife take care of him. But nonetheless, I get my workout done in the morning. This sets the tone for the rest of my day. I'm a morning person but I know not everyone is. As with everything else, you have to find what works for you.

A routine provides structure in your day and that's necessary to avoid getting overwhelmed by a long to-do list.

One of the elements of your routine has to be rehearsal or practice. When you go for an interview, or meet a client, or give a performance, you're selling yourself. What's going to separate you from everyone else? Why should Company A hire you and not the guy in the waiting area?

I go into nerd mode when I am rehearsing for an audition. I say this because I study my script like a nerd would study for a final exam – when I'm eating, when I'm working out (do nerds work out?), and even when I'm lying down to sleep (sometimes I even record myself reciting the lines and I listen to that in my earphones when I'm drifting off). I sit by myself and I read it over and over and over. Then I write it down in a notebook, over and over and over. And usually by then I have it memorized, or I'm off-book as we say in the industry, so I practise delivering my lines many different ways, over and over and over. I think you get my drift. And I do this every time I prep for an audition – it's my audition routine.

How to Prepare

It's nerve-racking going for an audition or job interview or asking for a raise. Beforehand, think of questions or objections the interviewers might use to make you stumble.

BTW: Learned from the Hired Assassin

As I mentioned before, it's important to be surrounded by people you respect, to help keep you sharp and to encourage you to aspire to greater heights. That's a great way to help you grow as an individual, personally and professionally. So when I noticed that I still was getting nervous at auditions even though my acting skills were advancing, I went to Clé Bennett, a friend and fellow actor, and asked him how he prepares for his auditions.

Clé's whole philosophy is that he is a hired assassin on a mission to murder a scene. When he goes into the audition, he has the positive mindset that he *knows* he already has the part. The audition is just to show the directors and producers that he can adapt to whatever direction they ask of him. Once you are prepared, he told me, you can conquer anything.

Clé showed me his preparation routine for auditions. First he takes his MP3 player and records his voice on all parts of the audition scene. Then he records just his dialogue. Then he records everyone else's dialogue and whispers his dialogue. *Then* he records everyone else's dialogue except his. Then he'd loop it on his MP3 player and go over it again and again. You don't have to understand it but this type of preparation is what has landed him some major TV and film roles, and it's made him one of the most sought-after black actors in Canada. He's also beat me out of a few parts, but I'm coming to get him!

"But Wes," you might be thinking, "if they're asking trick questions, how am I supposed to anticipate them?"

You have to research and rehearse.

When I started out shopping my demo tape to U.S. labels, even though I didn't know the right protocol in setting up meetings with record companies, I did know which specific labels to approach. I had researched what artists were on which labels, so I could approach the ones with the top rap artists. It would have been a waste of my time to drop off tapes, for example, to a label that represented only country artists. I had my elevator pitch ready because I knew exactly how I wanted my album to sound and even what I wanted the cover to look like. I knew precisely how my concept was going to be executed, because everything was all written down. If I needed to explain this to an executive at a label, I would be ready.

It was also important for me to not only be prepared to spit rhymes if I was put on the spot, but to be able to explain myself to record execs – fast. I had to be ready to let folks know what separated me from other MCs, and to let them know why they should sign me instead of someone else. I rehearsed my explanation of my concept and style over and over again in the mirror almost like I was rehearsing a new song. I was ready for any question they could throw my way.

A lot of young managers and upcoming recording artists come to me for advice and consultation about promoting their singles. Cats tell me they want to talk to radio programmers to play their new single, but they aren't sure whether they should shoot a music video to support the track. Instead of mapping out a plan, they're winging it, and that's a mistake many people make. It stunts their personal growth as well as the growth of the project. It doesn't matter if you're not a musician – you could be an engineer, a librarian, a carpenter, a professor – the same concept applies to everyone. You need to have a big picture . . . and a plan.

Prepare yourself for any possibility, because there's always going to be an element of the unknown.

Anticipate Obstacles

You also need to prepare yourself for any possibility, because there's always going to be an element of the unknown. No matter how carefully you've crafted or orchestrated your plan, there may be something that throws you off your game.

Don't allow yourself to get distracted or sidetracked during your big moment, and make sure you really observe the people you're addressing. When running your sales pitch through your head beforehand, practise it at least five different ways. That way, when it comes down to it, if the person isn't feeling you, or if he doesn't seem interested, you can adjust your approach on the fly. Watch out for body language. Is he looking directly at you, or does he keep glancing over your shoulder? Is she leaning slightly towards you in anticipation, or is she fidgeting and playing with her hair? These are some of the things that will help you tell if you've got their attention or if you need to shift gears.

In the summer of 2009, a few UFC fighters came to one of my shows in Montreal. They invited me to come to the gym the next day and watch UFC world champion Georges St-Pierre in a private sparring session. It was the last one before GSP and his crew flew to Las Vegas for the Saturday, July 11th fight with the fierce Thiago Alverez.

It was an honour to watch Georges finesse his skills before he headed to Vegas. Several top fighters flew in from France and the Dominican Republic to spar with him — one of them even looked like Alvarez. GSP and his crew were not messing around.

My dude was so prepared for the fight, it blew my mind. When I met him, I asked him how he felt. He smiled and said with his thick French-Canadian accent, "I'm ready. Nervous, but ready."

I don't think I've ever met anyone more humble than this guy. He was pouring sweat from head to toe after his sparring session, yet he still made time to say what up — and he honestly admitted that he was nervous about his upcoming fight. Even though he could beat the hell out of anybody in the world, he was totally peaceful and personable. In fact, it's probably *because* he knew he could beat the hell out of anybody that he was so quietly self-confident.

Nine days later, GSP won the match. I was amped to see that, especially since I had seen first-hand how hard he worked at it and how deserving he was of that win. I have no doubt his intense, constant physical and mental preparation, combined with his self-assurance and humility, set him up for success. All the hard work paid off when Alvarez raised GSP's hand to give him props.

Whatever you're doing – an interview, a performance, a sale – you want to be so prepared that you can tailor it to any personality. With preparedness comes confidence and ease. This means you can go with the flow, because you're not married to one style or even one outcome. You're open to different options and ideas. This way you're able to take more out of a situation.

Prepare Even More

In the spring of 2006, I got a call from Gail Harvey, the *Metropia* director who had made me almost want to quit acting years earlier. We'd stayed in touch, and she phoned me when she saw a music video I had done, the Classified video for "Hard to Be Hip Hop."

We talked about the video, and then I asked what projects she was working on. She told me about this George F. Walker TV show called *The Line*. I asked her if there were any parts I could play, and she said she'd see what she could do.

Next thing I knew, I had an audition for the part of a character named Andre Gilbert. He was as complex a character as any actor could want – good, bad, funny, dead serious, calm, violent – the whole spectrum. I was going to have to murder the audition.

With preparedness comes confidence and ease.

I prepared like mad, morning, noon, and night, until I became Andre. I asked some of my friends from *Metropia* to help me out by reading lines from the other parts and giving me feedback.

I found a studio down the street from where I was living in Vancouver. I had to put my audition on tape to send it electronically to the casting director. I asked my friend, Sean Bell, to come with me and read the other characters' lines for the audition. We had to start over a few times, because he lost concentration when I went into character. He couldn't believe how realistic I made Andre.

I got the part.

Learn from Your Friends

I first became friends with Clé Bennett, the "Hired Assassin," when I started filming *The Line*. He was one of the other leads in the show and had acted in the movie *How She Move*. He's a wicked actor, and what's most impressive to me is his focus.

He and I both knew we had to prove ourselves on the series. Our performances had to be *great*. Good was not good enough because to me "good" lives next door to "average." I mean, this series has serious acting folks, like Ed Asner (from *Lou Grant* and *The Mary Tyler Moore Show*), Linda Hamilton (Sarah Connor in *The Terminator*), and Sharon Lawrence (from *NYPD Blue* and *Desperate Housewives*).

Long story short, we nailed it! Our performances were dope, and I can confidently say that because our preparation was incredible. The more we worked on the show, the more respect we gained for one another. He didn't know too much about my acting ability before *The*

Good was not good enough because to me "good" lives next door to "average."

Line, but from the first day I was on set, he could see how committed I was.

It's funny how things change – Gail went from scrutinizing my wackness on *Metropia* to praising my performance on *The Line*. Just before we wrapped up, she hugged both me and Clé and said she'd never seen anyone prepare as hard as we did. That was one of those moments when all the hard work, getting back up from discouragement, paid off.

<<REWIND

Create a routine that will help you develop good habits and avoid distractions. Do your research, identify possible obstacles or objections, and practise overcoming them. Prepare, prepare, prepare! Then prepare some more.

Exercise 17: **More Prep Work to Help You With the Hurdles**

1. In your Vision Book, come up with a routine that will help you structure your days in order to be more efficient with your time. Make sure you account for everything you like to do on a regular basis – work out, respond to e-mails, go for coffee, etc. This will help you prioritize your tasks and allot time for the things you enjoy doing, as well as for the obligations you must do.

2. Think of an upcoming scenario where you might possibly face hurdles or tough questions. Divide your page in half and on the left side of the page, make a list of all the possible objections you might face. Then on the right side, beside the objection, write a rebuttal. This table will help you mentally prepare for the hurdles that otherwise might trip you up.

18: **CALLING AUDIBLES**

"Stay committed to your decisions, but stay flexible in your approach."

— ANTHONY ROBBINS

Those of you who are football fans probably already know what calling audibles means. Sometimes in a game, the quarterback calls a play in the huddle – but then when he gets to the line of scrimmage and takes a look at the defence, he calls a different play. What he's done is known as "calling audibles." It means adjusting your game plan on the fly, when things aren't going the way you expect.

When you've practised enough that you know your shit backwards and forwards, it's good to plan a few "audible calls" so that when something unexpected happens, you can make a few minor adjustments and still come out on top.

An example of how this worked for me was one time while filming *The Line*. I had a huge scene in which I beat up a punk-ass guy and all weekend I practised how I wanted to play the scene. I thought it would be cool to be totally calm as I was beating down this cat. I wanted to throw my punches while delivering my dialogue in a laid-back tone. I practised it other ways too, but this was my first choice.

Gail Harvey was directing the episode, and she was not feeling my choice for the scene. She pulled me aside and whispered in my ear, "Wes, I love you, but you're not doing this right. You're beating up this piece-of-shit kid who messed up your whole organization. You've got to kick his ass!" Because I practised the scene a bunch of different ways, I was able to adjust and go with the feel the director wanted. (I must admit that fight scene is great to watch.) In many cases, my initial idea for a scene might work, but it makes me feel good – and look good – when I'm flexible enough to call an audible.

<<REWIND

On the way to your destination, know that you'll encounter some detours. But when you know your shit inside out, you can plan some "audible calls" so if something unexpected happens, you have a few backup plans.

BTW: Listen to Your Career

I became friends with a wise man and musician named Larry Gowan after I remade a hit song of his. One of the best pieces of advice he ever gave me was, "Listen to what your career is telling you to do."

He told me how he came to be the piano player for the 1970s mega-group Styx — he was opening for them in Montreal when they had a falling out with their lead singer Dennis DeYoung. The other members approached Larry and asked him to join the band, and he said to himself, "On my own, I can do shows for a couple thousand fans. If I join this group, I can perform for hundreds of thousands of fans." His vision as a musician, at that point in his career, was to expand his international presence and joining Styx would allow him to do that. So although he was quite comfortable and things were going well for him as a solo artist, his career ambitions were pointing him in the direction of Styx. To choose not to join the group would be going against the signs.

When people don't listen to what their career is telling them — and many, many don't — they wind up feeling unsatisfied with their decisions.

At the time, I was dabbling in a few different business ventures and had two TV shows filming at the same time. It was a little overwhelming to say the least. When Larry told me, "Wes, listen to what your career is telling you to do," I did, and it was like a magic filter that prioritized things for me. I decided to focus on acting and it got much simpler and easier after that. Of course, I am still involved heavily in music, but concentrating on the acting has expanded my brand and made me a more dynamic person in the entertainment industry.

What's so funny about this story is that I'd said almost the same thing in one of my tracks on "Stick to Your Vision." The lyric "peep the composition" meant "listen to your own lyrics" or "listen to what you say." But it still took someone else to get me to *hear* it.

Exercise 18: **Take Stock**

1. Is there someone – a mentor, boss, or co-worker – whose advice you should be taking but have ignored because you didn't want to steer off-course? Use a page in your Vision Book to re-evaluate their suggestion and see if it just might actually enhance your work or project.

2. Are there skills you're lacking in some area of your career or profession? Make a list of these skills and figure out if it makes sense to try to sharpen them or if you should just quit while you're ahead and focus your energy on something you're better at. Be real with yourself. Will you get closer to your destination if you channel your energy elsewhere?

Sometimes you're going to need to call an audible in a much bigger way than in one scene or one job interview. Sometimes it's for your whole career.

Sol Guy manages international recording artist K-naan and some other artists, but his first vision was to be a rapper himself. The problem was, he had stronger skills in other areas. Actually, someone he really admired and respected finally told him, "Look, I think you'd be more successful as a manager."

He took the advice to heart and became one of the top, most-respected managers in Canadian hip hop.

Now he's taking it even further.

Sol created a TV show on the National Geographic Channel called "4Real," where he travels the world with celebrities to meet young leaders in different countries to raise awareness about poverty and illness. He couldn't have done that without his entrepreneurial skills — which he might not have gotten if he'd never taken a chance on being a manager. By understanding he needed to change his plan, he found areas of success that he would never have thought about before. He had to tap into a different part of that vision for people to see — for him to see — where he had to go.

Be open to the idea that once you're putting your plan in action, it may become clear that what you need is a different plan, which could take you to a higher level than you originally imagined.

THREE: DESTINATION

"Success is not the key to happiness.
Happiness is the key to success. If you love
what you are doing, you will be successful."

— ALBERT SCHWEITZER

Overleaf: Getting inducted into the Scarborough Walk of Fame. That's my dad behind me. (Photo by Jill Kitchener/*The Scarborough Mirror*, 2006)

TALKIN' WINDOWS: PART THREE

After lots of hard work, and a few bumps and bruises, you've persevered and finally made it through the window.

WINDOW NUMBER THREE:
So you made it through, huh?

YOU:
Yeah, I did. I finally did it.

WINDOW NUMBER THREE:
So how does it make you feel?

YOU:
Like a champ!

WINDOW NUMBER THREE:
I knew you would. You've officially arrived. You made it happen and I'm proud of you, son. But guess what?

YOU:
What's that?

WINDOW NUMBER THREE:
You're not finished yet. Now that you're here, you have a responsibility to enlighten the people you left behind. You have to teach them what you've learned. You have to help them through this window too . . . or even better, you can open the door for them.

YOU:
Thanks for the help, Mr. . . . umm, you never told me your name.

WINDOW NUMBER THREE:
Realization.

19: ARRIVAL

"Hard work truly does pay off! I started
a long time ago in hopes that this day
would come, where I could be recognized
for my hard work . . . on my abs."

— USHER

On the music tip, there were two moments that signalled to me I'd reached my destination. One was personal, the other public.

Private Symphony

One day, in August 1989, there was a knock at the door, and a UPS guy handed me a square package – copies of "Let Your Backbone Slide." It was the first time I was seeing my record for real. To me it was bigger than Christmas is to a kid. It was one of the most amazing feelings I've ever had. I couldn't believe I'd actually done it. I mean, I'd worked my ass off, I'd made things happen, and I realized this was the payoff – but it was still surreal. That record was like a trophy to me, and I carried it around the house with me all the time. I'd sit at breakfast eating oatmeal, spoon in one hand, "Backbone" in the other. I kept staring at my name, trying to comprehend the magnitude of this. I couldn't believe it was mine. I looked at the cover, and there was my name, but – you know when you say one word over and over again until it sounded strange, like it isn't a word? – that's what it was like. It was my name, but I couldn't fully appreciate that it was *me*.

On the cover was a black-and-white photo my dad had taken of me and DJ LTD. I sent that to the label and told them that was the cover I wanted. I didn't tell them I wanted my name in fluorescent pink, or to have the back cover in fuchsia – not the most masculine colours – but it bothered me for about two seconds before I thought, *Who cares? This is my damn record! I did it!* I held it in my hands, and I just stared at it. I put it in between other records on the shelf to see how it looked, moved it around, and then when I'd walk by, it would catch my eye, and I'd think, "Oh shit, that's my record!"

I was proud. It wasn't just vanity. Years earlier I'd told myself I was going to do this, and I did it, I made it happen. People had told me I was dreaming, that it was totally unrealistic. I'd lived through the opposition of my friends and family and through being hated by people who didn't even know me. I'd gotten lost in New York – and I mean that in all kinds of ways – and I found my way home. *I. Did. It.*

I'd come a long way since that photo of me, the one in my wallet, as a kid in a stupid red turtleneck with a fish on it. That kid would be proud of me!

Public Symphony

In November of 1989, Farley and I were hanging out at a club in Scarborough called Falcon's Nest. It was one of the places he and I would go to chill and kick it with our friends.

We were vibing to some beats and then Heavy D's joint "I Want Somebody to Love Me" came on. The track was one of the hottest hip hop records at the time; it featured Al B. Sure on the chorus. Farley and I were in mid-conversation when suddenly he stopped talking and his eyes widened. It only took a split second to know why. Underneath Al B. Sure's vocals, I heard the drum track of "Let Your Backbone Slide." I couldn't believe it. Was this real? Then I heard

When you think about what success looks like to you, think about what will mean the most to you.

the chorus of "Backbone" blend right in and Farley and I went ballistic. I'd never heard my song in a club before – *and* mixed in with a record from a huge U.S. artist. Heavy D. Maestro Fresh-Wes. *You've got to be kidding.*

All over the club, people were celebrating with us. They were amped and were wilding out, throwing their hands in the air and coming over to give us love. We were getting hugs and kisses from the ladies and pounds from the fellas. Needless to say, neither of us paid for another drink the rest of the night.

When you think about what success looks like to you, think about what will mean the most to *you*. To have the hottest DJ at one of Toronto's hottest clubs pick *my* song to mix in with Heavy D . . . In my neighbourhood, in my community, in my club – that was a breakthrough right there.

But it was the winter of 1991 that marked the arrival to my destination with an exclamation point. As I mentioned earlier, "Backbone" was a contender for Best Dance Recording at the Junos the previous year, but it didn't win. Well, this year (1991), I had received a total of five Juno nominations. And not only that, but CARAS had added a Best Rap Recording category to the Juno Awards, for which my album *Symphony in Effect* was nominated.

I can still remember how nervous I felt at the award show; I had a serious case of butterflies. My gear was mad tight though – I

BTW: Signals Marking Your Arrival

Chances are you know what will signal your arrival. It may not be as dramatic as hearing your song in a club or on the radio, but it will still be concrete: landing the job of your dreams, getting a promotion, winning a game – or getting off the bench for a game, raising a certain number of funds for an organization, and so on.

This is why, back in the beginning, I asked you to write out what success looked like to you. If you don't have that concrete goal, you may never feel like you've done enough or are successful enough. Goals, big or small, are important!

was rocking a fresh burgundy suit and I had a crisp high-top fade that my homie-slash-barber, 2 Rude, hooked up for me. When my name was announced as the winner of the Best Rap Recording, I was so high with excitement that it felt like I floated to the stage. My nerves seemed to have gotten the better of me, though, 'cause I forgot to thank my producers, Peter and Anthony, during my acceptance speech (I called them after the show to thank them and apologize at the same time), although I did remember to thank CARAS for acknowledging me and my genre of music. By the end of the night I had also collected a Juno for Best Video for "Drop the Needle." This solidified my arrival, as well as the arrival of hip hop in Canada. For me, that was success.

On the acting tip, the first time I really felt like I had made it was when one of the films I was in, *Poor Boy's Game*, screened at the Toronto International Film Festival. I was walking out of the theatre when it ended and I felt someone grab my arm. I turned around and looked up to see Donald Sutherland towering over me. And he said something I will never forget: "You were great." That meant a lot coming from him. At another event around that time, I ran into Sarah Polley, and after she had told me she knew all the words to "Backbone," she introduced me to her father as "Wes Williams." You might not see the magnitude of this so I'll break it down. I know damn well she knew of me first as Maestro Fresh-Wes, so the fact that she got past that and saw me as actor Wes Williams, that was huge.

I had arrived at my destination.

Surreality

Arriving at your destination can feel surreal and unbelievable. I mean, this is somewhere you wanted to be, something you worked towards achieving for months, years, or even your whole life. The feelings of pride and relief and gratitude that rush over you can be overwhelming. To say it's an emotional experience is an understatement – that's why you'll see even the toughest professional athletes cry when they win their sport's championship. It can also be an unusual and even uncomfortable feeling to suddenly have fans of your work, or for your product to be on back-order, or for your schedule to be full of appointments for months ahead.

The other side of it, too, is that you've gotten accustomed to the way life is, in pursuit of your vision, and when you arrive at your destination, most of your world changes. Maybe you no longer have to work at your day job or maybe you are now the boss. Maybe you can finally move out on your own or buy the dream house you've always fantasized about. Or maybe, like in my case, your arrival has brought some fame and notoriety.

A few months after "Backbone" was released, I was at the Square One Shopping Centre in Mississauga to do a signing. I was in a makeshift green room the record store had set up – basically the washroom with a vase of carnations on the sink – and Farley was standing outside. I leaned out to ask him something, and couldn't help but notice that the mall looked like a subway station at rush hour. I'd been in a fog for a few months, but I was pretty sure malls weren't usually wall-to-wall crowds.

"What's with all these people?" I asked Farley.

"The mall's been shut down," he said. *What, was there a bomb threat?* Farley seemed pretty casual about it, leaning back against a big bin full of records. His arms and legs were crossed, and he was watching all the people with half a smile on his face.

"Whaddaya mean, the mall's been shut down?"

"Too many people showed up," he said. I began to think he was tripping.

"Showed up for what?"

"You." He dropped it so casually that I wasn't sure what he'd said. Then he began laughing. "*You*, man!"

You've gotta be kidding me. I was used to fans screaming at shows, but this was something else. There were two huge security guards holding back a stampede of kids, mostly screaming girls, and all I could think was, *I'm glad I'm not working this event* – it was like I forgot I wasn't a security guard any more. Un-be-liev-able!

I sat down, and there were these girls screaming and crying – *crying* – like I was, I don't know, LL Cool J or something. I mean, I'm not belittling myself, I'm a good-looking brother, but I'm no pretty boy. I don't know, once you're on TV, get some popularity, people start treating you like you got better-looking. I went from "not bad-looking" to "good-looking" to "gorgeous"!

Once you're on TV, get some popularity, people start treating you like you got better-looking.

Honestly, I was numb, physically and emotionally numb, for a good few months. Sometimes it felt like I was having an out-of-body experience and I was watching this all play out from outside myself. I couldn't believe people were sweating me. Sometimes I just started laughing, because I didn't know what else to do.

And while laughing can be a great way to relieve some of the anxiety that comes with success, it's definitely not going to eliminate it permanently.

Don't Believe the Hype

Remember how I said I went numb when I found out I had caused a mall to be shut down? Some people don't go numb, but they wish they did. There's a reason so many famous people are drug addicts and alcoholics – it makes them feel less freaked out about what's happening.

The good news is that there are many ways to stay grounded in the midst of the crazy change that success and fame can bring.

I'm a spiritual person to some degree and I find it uplifting to pray and go to church. I pray all the time and for many different reasons – to give thanks, to bless my food, to ask for help, to ask for strength, for comfort – you name it, I've probably prayed for it. To me, praying is just talking to God, whom I believe to be the Higher Power. And I try to go to church when I can. To me, religion is a guide and spirituality is the goal. I know it's not for everyone but for me it gives me strength and makes me feel good.

I've seen people smoke away their ambition.

Although I don't meditate, I've heard from many

BTW: Addictions

It doesn't matter who you are, you have to have a clear head to get to your destination. That means staying positive and avoiding distractions. You can't control external factors/forces but the things you can control, you *need* to control. That's one of the reasons I avoid drugs – there are so many negative forces out there already, why add more to the mix? Trust me; I've seen way too many people in my industry fall off because of drugs – coke, heroin, and even weed (I've seen people smoke away their ambition).

If you're trying to be successful, you can't afford to get side-tracked. Don't get it twisted though – drugs aren't the only things that can knock you on your ass. Any vice can do that to you. Excessive drinking, gambling, partying, women/men, Internet chatting, whatever – those can all distract you from your plan if you spend too much time pursuing/ doing them.

If you're going to get addicted to anything, get addicted to your vision.

people that it can offer the same benefits as prayer. I've been told it helps keep you grounded and calm the mind. Call it prayer or meditation, all I know is that it's therapeutic to tap into your source.

Speaking of therapeutic, I find the gym a great way to relieve stress. Lifting weights helps me clear my mind because I get into a zone where I push myself so hard there's no room for

Get addicted to your vision.

any negative thoughts. But I admit there are times when I've gone to the gym with anxiety and it's limited my ability to push as much weight. It can be deflating and sometimes it makes me want to just go home, but I give myself a bit of a break and I will just lift lighter weights but do more reps. Even after an easier workout, I still feel rejuvenated. These are just a few pointers on the health tip that can help you stay grounded in spite of fame and prevent you from feeling like you have to numb out.

<<REWIND

You determine what success means *to you*. When you arrive at your destination, make sure you take time to reflect on your journey and to celebrate your accomplishment. Success or fame (or popularity) don't solve your problems, in fact, sometimes they can create more. It can be easy to turn to vices to escape fame or pressure, but it's in your best interest to find a healthy way to cope with the pressure and all the attention.

Exercise 19: **You've Come a Long Way, Baby**

1. Flip through your Vision Book to see how far you've come and all the planning and hard work you've done.

2. Picture yourself as the focus of a room full of people – they're staring at you, smiling at you, talking to you, making comments about you, taking pictures of you (not always at good times), hugging you, groping you . . . every reaction you can imagine. In your Vision Book, write down how you will respond when:

   • someone asks for your picture or autograph
   • someone compliments you
   • someone insults or criticizes you
   • someone asks you an inappropriate question

3. What techniques will you use to ground yourself when you're overwhelmed by your popularity and the spotlight? What activities do you find calming and uplifting?

4. What will you do when you are propositioned with alcohol, drugs, or sex? If you choose to welcome them, where do you draw the line?

20: COMPLIMENTS AND CRITICISMS

"I'm not into many compliments. Compliments are a distraction. People start telling you how good you are, and you stop working that hard. Then you become fat, lazy . . . so I don't live my life based on compliments."
— JIMI HENDRIX

Some people say you shouldn't read your reviews, but I do. I know some reviewers will show me love, and others won't, so I'm prepared for both. I don't take it personally. After all, I'm the one *doing* it, and they're the ones *watching*.

Every career has high and low points. I'm a huge Spike Lee fan. *Mo' Betta Blues* is my all-time favourite movie, but *Girl 6?* Not one of my favourites, and not necessarily what his fans were expecting, and he got criticized for it. But the thing is, he went out there and tried something different. *Girl 6* is not *Malcolm X.* But it wasn't supposed to be.

I get inspired watching how professional athletes bounce back from a bad play or game . . . or even from a bad season. A good example is Pro-Bowl quarterback Donovan McNabb. I have seen him get booed by his fans, reprimanded by his coach, benched, humiliated in the press – and still he'll return to take his team to the play-offs, all the while *smiling*. When he throws his touchdown passes and watches the time run out on the clock, it seems as if he manages to laugh at the fact that he got booed by his fans a few games earlier.

We have certain expectations of what people are going to do, and we all like different things. Same goes for critics. In every review or evaluation, especially of something artistic, there is an element of personal bias.

There have been times when a director or the producers told me what a great job I did on a scene and

Focus on doing great work and see the compliments as a bonus.

it's thrown me off my game when I was shooting the next scene. Instead of concentrating my efforts on how to make the scene great, I was thinking mostly of impressing the producers, hoping they'd tell me how wicked I was again – and that took my head out of the game.

This has happened to me in music as well. If fans or colleagues compliment me on a track, I have to be careful not to let it change how I approach the next one, creatively or technically. By focusing on "being liked," I can lapse into assimilation – trying to anticipate what my audience will like – rather than focusing on striving for innovation. And innovation is by far more creatively rewarding and more memorable.

Even if you're not in an artistic field, you'll still come up against this. Your boss likes your presentation, or you get a glowing performance review, and then instead of focusing on doing a great job, you focus on getting a raise or a promotion.

Compliments are addictive in that way. You get one, and you want more. Don't get me wrong, compliments by nature are constructive and can be good positive reinforcement that drives you forward; however, if your focus is only on trying to get more compliments, you're getting distracted and undermining yourself because your head isn't in the right space. Focus on doing great work and see the compliments as a bonus.

If you get sidetracked by compliments, you need to check yourself and go back to your original vision and your personal mission statement, which you created in Chapter 6. These will help remind you of the expectations you've set up for yourself (and not anyone else) and will help keep you true to them. Remember, that personal mission statement is there to keep you in alignment with your values – check in with it as often as you need to.

On the flip side, while your first response might be to get discouraged by criticism, you can also learn from it – and you should. But it's essential that you understand the difference between a constructive criticism and a plain old criticism because there's a big difference: one can be helpful while the other can be hurtful.

Constructive criticism is a critique that comes with advice on how to improve.

When my man DJ Greg was spinning for me and told me I was ahead of the beat and I needed to slow down, I didn't take offence to it. I took the opportunity to learn from it.

There's a saying that you must either decide not to believe your press at all or to believe the bad along with the good. It's not a selective thing. You can substitute "feedback" for "press" (and if it's from your boss, yeah, you probably do want to pay attention to the criticism, as long as it's constructive).

My friend Esai Morales, of *NYPD Blue* fame, watched my demo reel and said he noticed how I exploded in the scenes where I played angry and suggested that I might want to be a bit more subtle because that would give me more options for emotions in the aftermath. That's a lot different from when a viewer of *The Line* just straight up told me my character was too angry – that's just a criticism. And when someone criticizes or hates on you, you should just let it slide right off your back. Take a deep breath, and when you're calm, revisit that person's comments to find out if there's anything constructive there. A constructive criticism should be contemplated and used to step your game up.

Let's say your boss gave you a hard time over a project. A good boss will either tell you or help you figure out how to do a better job next time. A really good boss will acknowledge that mistakes are how you learn. But not all bosses are good, and fewer are *really* good.

So, be proactive and turn the criticism into constructive criticism. Acknowledge your mistakes and ask *for their advice* about what you can do differently next time. I emphasize "for their advice" because there's a difference between asking, "What do you want me to do?" and playing it politically by saying, "Based on your experience, what are some things I might do differently next time?" Not to mention you could score some points with your boss, because people are usually flattered when you ask for their opinion.

When it comes to compliments and criticisms, I have a "two-bin system" I use when dealing with them – they either go in the garbage bin or the recycling bin. If I can extract some positive advice that will help me improve, the compliment or criticism goes in the recycling bin to be revisited and reused. If the compliment or criticism doesn't offer an idea upon which to progress, or if it distracts me, it gets thrown in the trash bin. This helps my brain sort through all the information and prevent things from piling up. You might want to go ahead and adopt this system.

<<REWIND

Compliments and criticism can take your head out of the game. Appreciate the compliments, but stay focused on doing the best job you can – not on getting more compliments! Learn to distinguish between criticism and constructive criticism. If it's just a critical assessment without any advice, it's not helpful, so disregard it. If it's a critique along with suggestions, use it to improve.

Exercise 20: **Strategizing**

In your Vision Book, decide on a strategy for how you are going to deal with compliments, criticisms, and constructive criticism. Feel free to implement my two-bin system. For fun, you can even make it tangible and pick up two bins and label them – garbage and recycling. Write down the compliments and criticisms you receive and then throw them in the appropriate bin. At the end of each day (or however often you choose – just make sure it's often enough that the bins don't overflow), take the notes from the recycling bin and paste or copy them into your Vision Book. Then beside each note, write down the corresponding step you will take towards improvement. Then take the garbage bin, making sure you don't reread the notes, and trash the contents. Remember, the garbage in there is useless so there's no need to revisit it.

I'm quite proud of this system and think it's dope, but if it's not for you, go ahead and come up with your own strategy. The point of this exercise is simply for you to establish a consistent approach to dealing with compliments and criticisms to ensure you don't get distracted by them and waste too much time dwelling on them.

21: DON'T HATE THE HATERS

"I don't know the key to success, but the key
to failure is trying to please everybody."

— BILL COSBY

n January 1990, I was at the top of my game. I had just gotten off a cross-country tour, and both my single and album had recently gone gold. I was celebrating a huge milestone both for my career and for Canadian hip hop.

I went to see a show featuring MC Lyte. The place was packed. The DJ spotted me in the crowd, smiled at me, and yelled into the mic, "Maestro Fresh-Wes is in the house! Everybody make some noise!" This was the kind of moment you dream about when you're working your ass off. I stood there with a big smile on my face, ready to be acknowledged by the crowd.

I was waiting for cheers, but what I heard were the loudest boos you could imagine. *What the fuck is this?* Only two months earlier, my "Backbone" video had premiered on MuchMusic, and everybody had shown me love. *And now they're hatin' on me already?*

Damn, that stung.

It seemed that people had a hate on for me for the same reason they had loved me two months before: because I was on television everyday and my joints had even crossed over to commercial radio. This lack of love broke my heart for a minute, because I had worked so hard! Plus, I was the first hip hop artist in Canada to receive national acclaim and mainstream acceptance.

What's their problem!?

I acted like it didn't bother me, but I was dying inside – those cats were killing me. I was getting hated on before the term "hating on" was even used to describe jealousy and envy. To finally get to the highest pinnacle of success in my country and then to have my own people turn on me was deflating, to say the least.

It doesn't matter how successful you become, there will always be haters. Even when you're at the top of your game, you're going to get negative vibes. Keep in mind that the people who are ahead of you are usually not the ones hating on you – they're too busy mapping out their next steps. It's always the cats who are not where you are that will try to deflate you and take your positive energy.

Today, I can look back and laugh at that situation, and I understand it much better than I did back then. My community and my city had never experienced one of their own being so commercially successful, so they

It doesn't matter how successful you become, there will always be haters.

didn't know how to be supportive. When you grow up in an environment that doesn't expect you to succeed – where you're not *supposed* to be successful – your triumphs can breed envy. Whatever the reason is for the hate, and it's usually just jealousy and certainly *never* about you – it's got everything to do with the person or people hating on you – you can't allow yourself to dwell on it or internalize it.

During times like this, it's essential that you tap into your core, which you've defined with your personal mission statement (refer to Chapter 6). Visualize what you want to do and know that adversity is an obstacle you'll have to face regardless of where or who it comes from. Your tenacity, drive, and perseverance will one day even inspire the haters, and take it from me, that's a great feeling.

Seeing Beyond the Haters

For those of you who aren't musicians, you might be thinking, "Man, I don't have a hit song out – so why are haters on my case?" I'll tell you: Every environment has negative energy regardless of what type of profession or industry you're in. You can even find haters in church. You know, the gossipy people who are up in everybody's business and talk too much at the water cooler at work but still find time to sing in the church choir? If people see a quality in you they admire and they wish they had, and if they are not secure enough in themselves without that quality, they are going to resent you and hate on you.

Some people will continue to hate but others will get over it in time.

A few years ago at The Soul Choice DJ awards show in Toronto, I presented Ron Nelson with a Lifetime Achievement award. In his acceptance speech, he turned to me and said he was proud to see that the same cats who hated on me back in the day had grown into the men who shook my hand.

While I continued to hustle over the years, the haters saw my successes and failures – they followed me even more closely than my fans. Eventually, they had no choice but to respect me because they saw how hard I'd worked and persevered through adversity. I think this was an inspiration to a lot of them, because they saw me struggle just as much as they saw me succeed. Over time, hate knocks itself out. Just keep your "eyes on the prize," and *try* not to let negativity throw you off.

Easier said than done, right?

Then just remember this: Generally speaking, the most successful people don't waste their time complaining or worrying about what other people are doing or not doing because they are too busy planning their next mission. Complaining really only stunts your growth and distracts you from what you should be focusing on. It's hard not to complain sometimes, especially when things aren't going the way you want them to, but know that complaining will suck up all your energy and you won't have anything left to put towards your vision. Trust me on that one.

With regard to the haters, just try to ignore them and don't expect them to change. They may change on their own, maybe not. You have to accept people for who they are, not who *you* think they should be. Just because you and I are inspired and driven to succeed doesn't mean everybody else is, and when you put expectations on other people, you set yourself up for disappointment. This is the flip side of what I talked about in the "Expectation" section. You don't want people putting expectations or labels on you, so don't do the same thing to them.

It's partly the Golden Rule – treat others as you want to be treated – but it's also about looking outside your own realm. You're on a certain level, and you're on a path to reach a higher echelon; you can do this because you're inspired and motivated and capable of excellence. But not everybody is as motivated and inspired as you are. In fact, a lot of people aren't. Whether it's lack of talent, low expectations they've internalized from others – or whatever – not everyone has tapped into their vision – not everyone wants to. Who knows? Maybe that person you're picturing will read this book, get motivated, and surpass you. You can't control what anybody else does, now or in the future. You can only control your own actions. So really just kick your own butt.

Complaining really only stunts your growth and distracts you from what you should be focusing on.

<<REWIND

You will always encounter haters. Their animosity towards you has nothing to do with you and everything to do with them. Don't set expectations for them and that includes expecting them to change. Be true to your values and your vision and keep plugging away. Who knows, maybe one day they might even surprise you and shake your hand.

Exercise 21: **Buzz Words**

On a page in your Vision Book, compile a bunch of words and images that help you refocus your thoughts on your accomplishments, as well as on your new aspirations. Posted on a bulletin board I have ticket stubs from award shows, cover pages of scripts from projects I've landed, and flyers from previous concerts I've done. Whenever there's negative energy thrown at me, I look at these images to help me focus on what's important. Your buzz words and images will become symbols of your successes in life.

22: HUMILITY IS A SKILL

"It was pride that changed angels into devils;
it is humility that makes men into angels."
 – ST. AUGUSTINE OF HIPPO

"Humility is a skill" is an expression I heard in church from a pastor I really respect named Pastor Orim Meikle. It stuck with me because I work in two industries where to have a big ego is normal and almost expected. Being an MC seems to give you the right to stick your chest out. A lot of times it's about fronting – you develop an alter ego that doesn't seem to leave after you're done recording. A lot of MCs never stop performing; they front and act like their life is a damn music video. The same thing goes in the acting industry most times. Although I've met some solid folks who have become lifelong friends, I can't tell you how many divas and hot shots I've met through acting.

When you succeed with your vision – become a manager or executive, a community leader or well-known artist or actor – you have choices about how to conduct yourself. That becomes part of your reputation, your brand – your legacy – so before you power trip, consider the consequences.

Humility, which means being modest about your accomplishments and acting the opposite of arrogant, connects you with everyone, while arrogance puts you on a pedestal and causes division. Although you may not see how arrogance can hurt others, it's based on the assumption that you're better than the next person and that therefore they are less than you. Respect is a human right and everyone is deserving of it, regardless of their status. Always treat people as equals and give them the respect they deserve.

Just because you might be smarter or richer or prettier doesn't make you better than anyone else – it simply makes you smarter or richer or prettier. And I got news for you, for all the people you're richer, smarter, and prettier than, there are just as many people out there who are richer, smarter, and prettier than you. And I have to point out, that besides being superficial qualities, all those things can be fleeting. Just think where you would be if you lost those things – you would still be you, and what's left is the core of you, the enduring qualities that will define you. So keep that in mind, too, the next time you're feeling yourself too much.

Before you power trip, consider the consequences.

Conductin' Thangs . . . Like Yourself

I talked about mentors earlier, and when it came to the "fame" part of my career, I couldn't have learned more than I did while doing shows with Ice-T and Public Enemy. Ice gave me indirect media training; Chuck D taught me how to conduct myself with fans, stage crew, opening acts – everybody. These guys are consummate professionals. They'd been doing it a while, and I have no doubt their careers have lasted as long as they have because people like working with them. They set the standard, in my mind, for **Humility connects you with everyone and arrogance puts you on a pedestal.** how iconic artists are supposed to act. Over the years, as I met popular artists who were pricks, I found their arrogance comical because I had met two of the biggest hip hop stars ever (who were a lot nicer on the mic than these guys) and they were the realest dudes. I appreciated Chuck D and Ice-T even more for this.

Another thing: these brothers not only appreciated their fans but they also had love for their touring and stage crews and their opening acts. For us musicians, fans are the reason we're successful – or famous – in the first place. Our road, stage, and house crews (usually) make us look and sound good, and they do all the heavy lifting – literally –so we can save our energy for a show. The opening acts are kind of like the receptionist at a big company – they're just starting out, but you'd better respect them on your way up, because when you're on the way down, they might own the company.

Ice and Chuck had a genuine interest in hip hop from around the world. They liked meeting new people, and they made each person feel special in their presence. They might've been the famous ones, but talking to them, you'd never know it – they were mad humble.

What's so funny is that, from the outside, you might never guess that these guys were so laid-back. We're talking Ice-T around the time of "Cop Killer," and PE, whose lyrics are arguably the most politically charged of our era. The thing is, they defined what hip hop evolved into after the embryonic, simplistic party records of the late 70s to early 80s. That's a topic for another whole book, but I just have to say that taking the rage that black folks felt and channelling it into music displaying sonic fury – that was pure genius.

Being humble is also about understanding that you're not the centre of the universe. It's important to look around and see what's going on in the world beyond your doorstep.

It was through my tour with Public Enemy and my tour with Ice-T that I learned a lot more about black history and black-American social commentary. PE's songs were very political, and Ice-T was the first West Coast rapper I'd ever heard. Hip hop is very territorial and was created in New York, so a rapper out of California was almost as foreign a concept as a rapper from Canada – 'cause we both weren't from New York. All the black

Without humility, our egos and false pride can easily contaminate our mind and have a negative hold on our spirit.

social issues they rhymed about were new to me, and definitely important stuff. Those brothers indirectly helped me understand my story.

What I learned from PE and Ice is this: Respect and be cool with everybody, because they are the ones who make your success happen. That's how you should move, and it works in every field – and in life. If you can't be genuinely respectful, practise until you get good at it. And seriously, if PE, one of the most prolific hip hop groups of all time, can be humble, anyone can!

Invisible Man

In 1999, I was on a major comeback. "Stick to Your Vision" was doing well on radio, and my career seemed to be on its way back up – thankfully.

The boy band 98 Degrees was touring the major cities in Canada, and through a series of connections, I was asked to open for them. I know: 98 Degrees. Maestro. One of these things is not like the other. But it was a good opportunity to lay the groundwork for a future solo tour, and it would definitely expose my music to an audience who wouldn't have otherwise heard it.

Now, I can't lie. I wasn't really feeling 98 Degrees, but I knew the benefits outweighed having to hear "Invisible Man," their hit single, twenty times.

The first show was in Ottawa. My crew and I got to sound check only to find out that 98 Degrees already had an opening act, some chick by the name of Jessica Simpson. I'd go on second. *Second!? What the hell is this?* I watched this blonde teeny-bopper sound check for her full hour . . . then she sound checked through what was supposed to be my time slot. No worries. I was a professional. I knew that once I got on that stage, everybody would forget about blondie.

The thing is, I didn't know till she was finished that there wasn't time for my sound check. *Who does this girl think she is, pushing me out of my sound check?* I wanted to confront the tour manager about the lack of respect I was getting but I couldn't because there wasn't enough time. I had to rush back to the hotel to get changed and back to the venue in time for the show. Then there was mad traffic. I showed up five minutes late, and 98 Degrees' tour manager said I couldn't perform. *What? Didn't they know that I didn't need to be on this tour and that they were lucky to have me?*

Words can't express how heated I was. Farley was pissed, too.

I was a platinum-selling artist, whose popularity had shut down a mall and I couldn't believe the disrespect I was getting on this tour. I was so vexed I contemplated quitting and leaving them high-and-dry. But once I let off some steam I realized it wasn't my tour and I wasn't in the position to be calling shots. Sure, we were touring Canada, and I was more established nationally than both those artists combined, but they were running the show, not me. The bottom line is that we were late. We just had to swallow that pill and our pride. If I'd caused any beef, I would have been kicked off the bill, and although I knew I was an asset to their tour, the exposure I was getting was too important to lose.

I stayed calm and kept it moving, despite my bruised ego. This situation was very humbling for me because I learned I had to play my position. Nonetheless, by the end of the tour, Farley and I realized that the fellas of 98 Degrees were some real cool cats. So was Jessica Simpson and her family. Even the tour manager seemed less scary now. He wasn't the nicest guy, but he was just doing his job. It wasn't personal.

Without humility, our egos and false pride can easily contaminate our mind and have a negative hold on our spirit. I've learned through experience that when your heart and mind are weighed down with negative energy, it's really tough to think clearly – you run the risk of becoming super sensitive and your perception can become skewed.

<<REWIND

Regardless of the success or the status achieved, nobody is superior to anyone. Humility is a skill you need to add to your arsenal and practise everyday.

Exercise 22: **Humility Is in the House**

1. Learn the name of someone new every day for a week. There are people you see everyday, or almost everyday, that you never talk to. It could be the person who makes your coffee, another passenger on the subway, the cleaner in your building. Ask them their name, or read it off their nametag, and introduce yourself. Be sure to greet them by their name every time you see them.

2. Say thank you. Just like the example above, there are people you encounter everyday whom you might not recognize for their contributions. Go out of your way to take the time to say thank you: Thank you for clearing my tray; Thank you for taking out my garbage; Thank you for making such a wicked sandwich. Make it your mission everyday to say thank you to someone deserving . . . and that includes your loved ones, too.

23: PASS IT ON

"Successful people are always looking for opportunities to help others. Unsuccessful people are always asking, 'What's in it for me?'"

— BRIAN TRACY

Call it what you want, being a role model, example, inspiration, but people look up to you when you've reached a level they're trying to conquer. That's why it's important to stay on point and to continue to inspire people directly or indirectly with your words and actions. You don't have to wait till you reach your destination – at any point, you can share what you know or have gone through. But when you realize your vision, then it's definitely time.

I was in church with my family one day in 1989, just after my first album was released. After the service, a kid asked me for my autograph. As I was signing it, his father leaned over and whispered into my ear, "Don't mess this up." I would have rather heard "Congratulations," but I knew where he was coming from. His son looked up to me, and I felt a burden of responsibility.

I never forgot that father whispering in my ear. As one of very few young, famous black men in Canada, the pressure was on me to not mess up.

The more successful you become, the more pressure society puts on you: the pressure to not "screw up"; the pressure to be increasingly successful; the pressure to not let down your community, your city, or your country. Your own mind becomes a pressure-cooker as well: the pressure of knowing that there are people out there who are going to hate you for no reason other than your success; the pressure of envious folks who want you to fail so they can take your place; and above all, the pressure of not disappointing people, especially those you care about. All of these are expectations, positive or negative, and it's just as important not to internalize these implied expectations as it was when you first started out. Remember: You can't control what others think, say, do, or feel. All you can control are your own thoughts and actions. Keep in mind what you're looking for in life, and don't get overtaken by negative energy.

> You don't have to wait till you reach your destination – at any point, you can share what you know or have gone through.

I don't really like the expression "role model" because I think it implies you're playing that *role*, and you become like a politician, allowing yourself to be put on a pedestal and then trying to balance on it. You can wind up believing your own hype, and that's dangerous territory. If you're a role model, you have to walk on eggshells, because the minute you slip up, you're not just disappointing yourself; you're disappointing those who had high expectations of you, and at the same time you're fulfilling the negative expectations others had of you. But I guess the title of "role model" comes with the territory of success and fame. Call it what you want, you need to take this responsibility seriously.

It feels good to know you've said or done something that helps another person. That's why I do speaking engagements – it's passing on what I've learned, and making that difference in another person's life just feels good. It's not about being a "role model." It's simple: Just talk to people. Speak honestly, speak from your heart, and the right words will come out.

Remember my man Marving who said, "I tricked my mind"? When he told me that story, I said, "You have to go back to the people you worked with at the gas station. Show them how far you've come; show them that you wanted more, went after it, and achieved it – and you're continuing to aim higher." The point is, people need to know that others in the same situation have managed to overcome certain challenges. Your story can help inspire others. If Marving doesn't go back to see his old coworkers, chances are they may never know it's even *possible* for them to reach higher.

There's never a wrong time to thank people who have inspired and motivated you along the way. And just as

There's never a wrong time to thank people who have inspired and motivated you along the way.

arriving at your destination is definitely time to start sharing what you know, it's also time to start showing gratitude (if you haven't started already), to let people know what their words or actions meant in your life. Everyone appreciates hearing that they've made a difference to someone else – like I said, you never know who you're going to inspire, and it's such a good feeling when you find out you've had a positive impact on someone.

No matter what field you're in, take time to thank your mentors and even the people who gave you "tough love" – for me, people like Gail. It makes them feel good, and it makes you feel even better.

<<REWIND

It's never too early to start sharing what you've learned with others. Share your knowledge, speak honestly, and expect nothing in return. Remember how much it meant to you when others shared their experience. Be sure to thank those who have inspired and helped you along the way.

Exercise 23: **Saying Thank You in a Meaningful Way**

1. You have learned valuable lessons along the path to your destination that could be helpful to others who are on the same journey. What venues can you use to help pass on the knowledge you have? Can you become a mentor at work? Can you teach a class or be a coach? Can you speak on a panel? Can you volunteer at a community centre? Brainstorm in your Vision Book how to find a way to take your knowledge and pass it on.

2. Make a list of all the people who have helped you along the path to your destination. Send them thank-you cards or e-mails – or better yet, keep it ol' school and call them on the phone to thank them personally.

24: **KEEP IT MOVING**

*"There's still plenty to do. I think I'll never
run out of things to accomplish, as long as
I'm alive, because there's so much to learn,
and so much to do. I always feel like I have
so much further to go, personally, spiritu-
ally, emotionally, mentally, and physically."*
                    – QUEEN LATIFAH

You're going full throttle on Plan A, and while
you're doing A, you're learning about different
things, learning about yourself, and you think,
"Maybe I'd like to try B someday." As I was doing my
music, I was meeting people, evolving as a musician,
learning about other things that I could possibly do. In
other words, I wasn't specifically thinking of being an
actor, because I was full throttle into music. But because
of that experience, I developed a work ethic and a tem-
plate of what it takes for me to be successful. From that,
I decided I had to try something else to further my skills

and to evolve as an artist and an individual. As an actor, I've found out new things about myself. Who knows what's next?

Movin' on Up

"Stick to Your Vision" is a cycle, a spiral that will lead you higher and higher. When you reach your destination, it's time to aspire to further greatness. Build on the skills you've developed, and focus on developing new ones.

When I filmed *The Line*, I thought, "Damn, I did a good job – and now I want to do better." I did a killer scene with Sharon Lawrence. Bring on Will Smith! My expectations of what I can do have raised. I'm not trying to be *as good as* anyone else, I'm trying to be *my best*. The beauty of it is that you're doing it for yourself. You're doing it to see how far you can go.

> When you reach your destination, it's time to aspire to further greatness.

You have to continue to strive for greatness. If you strive to be great, and you end up being good, you can live with that. If you strive to be just good and you miss, that means you're average and that won't push you to a higher echelon. Good lives right next door to average, and I don't know about you but that's not where I want to live. I'm not trying to be good; I'm trying to be great.

Transitioning

My transition began when I decided to give acting a shot. First thing: I wrote down my vision for acting and created a plan. In 1998, while I was touring to support my album *Built to Last*, I was thinking of ways to expand my brand and diversify my career. I wasn't nineteen any more, and though I would always be involved in the music industry, there were other paths I wanted to explore. I researched the top acting coaches in Toronto and started taking acting classes. Although I had been performing as an MC for years and had become quite comfortable in front of an audience, my performance as an actor needed work.

And even after a decade's worth of work in TV and film, people in the industry still don't expect my acting skills to be on a high level. It can be frustrating, but I just continue to focus on doing what I have to do to prove myself. I had to work extra hard to show them I wasn't one of those cats who just wanted to take a limo from the recording studio straight to a wardrobe fitting for my latest film and then to a club to party till all hours.

If my transition had been into producing music or managing artists, I would've already had credibility. But it wasn't, so I had to work my ass off – again – to earn respect.

I took basic classes first – in acting, auditioning, on-camera acting, and then more advanced courses. I also studied by watching classic movies with Jack Lemmon, Jack Nicholson. I studied acting as intensely as I had studied music. I went to Queen Video, an independent video store in Toronto where I know the staff knows their movie history, and asked them to recommend some movies that showed killer performances. I asked them for little-known films, which made it much more interesting a project for me. I learned from some of the movies and performances that the masses never heard of but that are just as dope as the big-budget Hollywood films. This is the same thing I used to do when I was starting out in music – I would get suggestions on obscure records from the people working at the smaller record shops.

It took time, patience, and hard work to earn industry respect – especially since singers and rappers aren't generally taken seriously when they try to leap onto the big screen or small screen. But by preparing as thoroughly as I did, I showed them I was serious.

Not only did I show them I was serious: I showed them I was talented. I'm slowly but surely getting respect from the producers, directors, and actors who work with me, and now I'm getting respect from the industry (don't get it twisted, it doesn't mean everybody in the industry is feeling me) – at the time I'm writing this, I just received my first Gemini Award nomination (the Canadian equivalent to a Primetime Emmy Award). To say that I'm excited is an understatement. When I got the congratulatory e-mail from my agency informing me I had been nominated for "Best Performance from an Actor in a Supporting Role in a Dramatic Series" for my role as Andre on *The Line*, I can't lie, I jumped up and down like a little kid, much like I did at the club the first time I heard "Backbone" being played. To earn this respect and acknowledgment from my peers in the industry is huge to me, especially since I come from a music background and had to work extra-hard to be taken seriously as an actor.

While I appreciate the love and acknowledgement, I don't take it for granted. I worked my ass off and I still do, on each and every project.

I'm still hustling harder than ever, acting, performing, doing speaking engagements, being a father and husband, and now writing a book. The higher up the spiral you go, the more work it is – but the more fun you'll have by taking on new challenges and endeavours!

What I'm saying here is that no matter where you come from, what your past is, or where you are now, if I can make it happen, you can make it happen. Remember that no matter who you are, nobody wants to see you be more successful than you want to see it yourself. It's up to you to have faith in yourself, stay focused, and above all else, Stick to Your Vision.

<<REWIND

Continue to strive for growth and greatness. The skills you have acquired through previous experience and work can be used in other arenas as well. Go with the flow and allow for natural progression in your life and your career. Once you're at your destination, and if you decide you'd like to pursue another interest, start from the beginning, set your intention, and map out a plan. Remember to set *your* true expectations and know that the transition will take work. Above all else, have faith in yourself and Stick to Your Vision.

Exercise 24: **Stay Fresh**

1. Take a page in your Vision Book to make a list
   of "transferable skills and habits" you can take
   from your previous or current realm and implement in your new one. For example, through
   working on my music, I learned the importance
   of repetition. In order to remember all the lyrics
   to my songs, I had to constantly repeat them to
   myself. Then, after I'd memorized them, I would
   work on my flow and syncopation. Applying that
   same process to acting, I quickly became comfortable memorizing scripts. Because I had a
   strong reference point, I had an advantage over
   many people. It's always great to bring previous
   life lessons with you as you go along and to apply
   them wherever you can.

2. Do some research to figure out if there's a class
   you can take or a related organization you can
   volunteer with to get some experience and credibility in your new endeavour. Make a list of the
   possibilities in your Vision Book and determine
   which one best aligns with your personal mission statement (see Chapter 6). Then . . . do it.

3. Create a timeline: It takes time to learn before
   you can really establish yourself in a new career
   or endeavour. It will probably take even longer
   to be taken seriously by your peers and to get the
   props you think you deserve. Creating a timeline

with specific goals and dates will help keep you on track and remind you that you have to take your journey step by step. So go ahead, get out your Vision Book and make that timeline.

SUGGESTED READING

The following is a list of some books I have found motivational and I think you will too. Some of them are purely inspirational and help to refocus your perception when you're in need of a good boost. Some of them are biographical and I always find it uplifting to read about other people's trials, tribulations, and revelations. Some of them are straight up business books that will give you practical advice on how to start or improve your career. All of them are in keeping with the same universal lessons I have learned and have shared with you in this book. Hit up your local bookstore or library and check them out.

Ali, Muhammad and Hana Yasmeen Ali. *The Soul of a Butterfly: Reflections on Life's Journey*. New York: Simon and Schuster, 2004.

Angelou, Maya. *Wouldn't Take Nothing for My Journey Now*. New York: Random House, 1993.

Baber, Anne and Lynne Waymon. *Make Your Contacts Count: Networking Know-how for Business and Career Success*. New York: AMACOM, 2002.

Canfield, Jack and Janet Switzer. *The Success Principles: How to Get from Where You Are to Where You Want to Be*. New York: HarperCollins, 2005.

Coelho, Paulo. *The Alchemist*. San Francisco: HarperOne, 1973.

Comm, Joel, Anthony Robbins, and Ken Burge. *Twitter Power: How to Dominate Your Market One Tweet at a Time*. Hoboken, NJ: Wiley, 2009.

D, Chuck. *Chuck D: Lyrics of a Rap Revolutionary*. Edited by Yusuf Jah. Beverly Hills, CA: Off Da Books, 2006.

Darling, Diane. *The Networking Survival Guide: Get the Success You Want by Tapping Into the People You Know*. New York: McGraw-Hill, 2003.

Dyer, Wayne W. *The Power of Intention: Learning to Co-create Your World Your Way*. Carlsbad, CA: Hay House, 2004.

Garvey, Marcus and Bob Blaisdell. *Selected Writings and Speeches of Marcus Garvey*. Mineola, NY: Dover Publications, 2004.

Graham, Stedman. *Build Your Own Life Brand!: A Powerful Strategy to Maximize Your Potential and Enhance Your Value for Ultimate Achievement*. New York: Simon & Schuster, 2001.

Graham, Stedman. *You Can Make It Happen: A Nine-Step Plan for Success*. New York: Simon & Schuster, 1997.

Harper, Hill. *Letters to a Young Brother: MANifest Your Destiny*. New York: Gotham Books, 2006.

Hay, Louise L. *You Can Heal Your Life*. Santa Monica, CA: Hay House, 1984.

Hicks, Esther and Jerry Hicks. *The Law of Attraction: The Basics of the Teachings of Abraham*. Carlsbad, CA: Hay House, 2006.

Holyfield, Evander and Lee Gruenfeld. *Becoming Holyfield: A Fighter's Journey*. New York: Atria Books, 2008.

Holzner, Steve. *Facebook Marketing: Leverage Social Media to Grow Your Business*. Indianapolis, IN: Que, 2008.

Klauser, Henriette Anne. *Write It Down, Make It Happen: Knowing What You Want – And Getting It!* New York: Scribner, 2000.

Obama, Barack. *Dreams from My Father: A Story of Race and Inheritance*. New York: Crown, 1995.

Owens, Jesse. *Blackthink: My Life as Black Man and White Man*. New York: Morrow, 1970.

Poitier, Sidney. *The Measure of a Man: A Spiritual Autobiography*. San Francisco HarperSanFrancisco, 2000.

Robbins, Anthony. *Awaken the Giant Within: How to Take Immediate Control of Your Mental, Emotional, Physical and Financial Destiny!* New York: Simon & Schuster, 1992.

RZA, The. *The Tao of Wu*. New York: Riverhead Books, 2009.

Silber, Lee. *Self-Promotion for the Creative Person: Get the Word Out About Who You Are and What You Do*. New York: Three Rivers Press, 2001.

Tracy, Brian. *Maximum Achievement: Strategies and Skills That Will Unlock Your Hidden Powers to Succeed*. New York: Simon & Schuster, 1995.

Washington, Denzel. *A Hand to Guide Me*. Des Moines, IA: Meredith Books, 2006.

West, Kanye and J. Sakiya Sandifer. *Kanye West Presents Thank You and You're Welcome*. West Hollywood, CA: Super Good LLC, 2008.

Williamson, Marianne. *A Return to Love: Reflections on the Principles of A Course in Miracles*. New York: HarperCollins, 1992.